MW00629381

Practical Play

the Heart-Centered Way

Practical Play
the Heart-Centered Way

A Complementary
Play Guide to

Little Book of Big Potentials

Melissa Joy Jonsson

HEART-FIELD
PRODUCTIONS

Published by Heart-Field Productions Inc.
Seattle, WA 98136
info@mjoyheartfield.com

© 2015 by Melissa Joy Jonsson

All rights reserved. Printed in the United States of America. No parts of this book may be used or reproduced in any manner whatsoever without written permission, except in the case of brief quotations embodied in critical articles and reviews. For information, please contact the author directly at info@mjoyheartfield.com.

19 18 17 16 15   1 2 3 4 5

ISBN: 978-0-9915346-7-8 (Kindle)
ISBN: 978-0-9915346-6-1 (pbk)

M-Joy Fields, M-Joy Logo, Spiralglyphics, and the Spiralglyphics Circular Design are all trademarks of Heart-Field Productions Inc.

Library of Congress Control Number: 2015920666

Contents

Reading Guide

Practical Play the Heart-Centered Way is an experiential play guide intended to complement the teachings shared in *Little Book of Big Potentials: 24 Fields of Flow, Fulfillment, Abundance, and Joy in Everyday Life*. Although the practices in which you are about to engage can be applied effectively based only on the information shared herein, ideally this play guide is designed to expand on and enhance experiences of the 24 Fields shared in *Little Book of Big Potentials*. Please refer to Little Book of Big Potentials for a more comprehensive understanding of each Field and a more in-depth explanation of the science of heart-centered awareness and interactive reality creation.

Come PLAY and In-Joy!

Melissa Joy

$\mathcal{F}$101

F101. Heart Field. Coherency. Inner Dominion.

A heart field is a Love Sphere that is connected to everything. The field of the heart carries key codes for accessing the eternal now and also unlocks our individual and shared life purposes. The heart field is a gateway into all that IS, was, and may ever be. When we are living and loving from the field of the heart, we are true Heartists capable of creating and manifesting True Authentic Desires into actual experiences.

The field of the heart is an opening into truth as unity. Although the field of the heart is transpersonal in nature, it is very personal to each one of us, for within the field of the heart is everything we need to know to live extraordinary, empowered, meaningful lives. The field of the heart contains an inner navigation system, a GPS pointing the way to our own true north in all experiences. The

LENKA HORAVOVA/SHUTTERSTOCK

unlimited field of the heart always knows what the limited mind may have forgotten.

Living and experiencing from the field of the heart is easy, once we stop living and experiencing any other way. Consistently living from the field of the heart enables us to be our True Authentic Selves and supports True Authentic Relating. As the field of the heart does not take things apart, the experience of being in the field of the heart can be very unifying. We may experience ourselves as completion. We may experience ourselves as our true essence of love, void of programming. We may experience self-acceptance and authenticity.

We may experience ourselves in a form of preexperience, as unconditional love in a preconditioned essence. We may experience consciousness potential before that potential is an expression or distinction. Living from the field of the heart gives us access to ease as grace in all that we relate to, encounter, and experience.

Trying to understand the experience of the field of the heart from the mind can be limiting.

4

The mind compartmentalizes experience from a singular perspective, whereas the field of the heart is devoid of perspective and includes all perspectives as part of itself. The mind is a delineating processor that cannot comprehend the vast, boundless nature of the field of the heart and our true essence as unconditional love. Thus trying to understand the field of the heart from the mind can hinder our ability to Be, Live, and Love from the field of the heart. Allow for understanding to grow from experience. Experience being in the field of the heart, and true knowing as wisdom will gently reveal itself to you and through you.

Allow yourself to be guided in a playful manner away from thoughts, programs, expectations, and even beliefs. Allow yourself to be swept away by the sheer magnificence of our infinitely fractal nature. Allow yourself to move into a journey of heart-centered awareness.

Experience the boundless truth of our core essence as we PLAY together in the field of the heart. There is no preparation necessary for this journey into the field of the heart. You may come exactly as you are. You are ready for *Practical Play the Heart-Centered Way.*

The field of the heart is our portal into a sea of infinite potential, a vast, ever-expanding ocean of potentiality from which all waves of possibility swell up and merge into the shoreline of our reality. This ocean of boundless potential is both within us and surrounding us. This love is both within us and surrounding us.

One of my favorite ways to connect to the field of the heart and experience the sea of infinite love is by visiting the ocean in my awareness. I may lose all track of time as I reflect on the beauty of the magnificent, expansive sea: an ocean that spans far beyond the discernible horizon.

To me the ocean is a beacon for Field 101, Heart-Centered Awareness. Field 101 supports our ability to consistently access heart-centered awareness in all endeavors. When I want to signal Field 101, to drop into the field of my heart, I will often see the ocean in my mind's eye. I find myself naturally in the field of the heart while watching waves, feeling into each wave as a different possibility. I notice the beauty of each unique wave. There is always symmetry to each wave-form coupled with an asymmetry—spiraling curvatures that seemingly guide a wave's movement from a unified ocean of potential to distinct expression. As a wave breaks upon the shore, for a moment the wave appears separate from the sea. Then, as soon as now, each wave always returns to the undivided sea from which it came. Even as the waves flow to shore and quench the distinct yet interconnected granules of the soft sand, there is no point from which that wave is not always a whole part of the sea.

We are the same. We have emerged from a sea of limitless, undifferentiated consciousness poten-tial, as unconditional love, to express our indi-

CHRISVANLENNEPPHOTO/SHUTTERSTOCK

viduality, and yet we are always connected to an implicate order of the undivided flowing sea of All. We are still All experiencing All as individual. Infinite potential. Infinite expressions. Infinite distinctions. Infinite you.

A wave that merges with particles of sand is still connected to the ocean. We as individuals are still a whole part of the undivided sea of love from which we came. The field of the heart is that eternal connection. The field of the heart is that remembering. The field of the heart is that presence and experience. This space of grace is where a drop of water meets the eternal sea. The field of the heart is where choice meets possibility. The field of the heart is where individual perspective merges with that which is devoid of perspective and includes all perspectives as part of itself. The field of the heart is where nothing meets everything. The field of the heart is the truth of whom we are.

To me, watching the ocean is like watching love's movement in flow, as the creative intelligence of the universe. The truth of beauty as unity spirals as waves of possibility. Love is the Eternal Spiral. WE are love eternally spiraling in golden means through waves of grace. The golden mean spiral has no beginning and no end. This spiral is where infinite potential meets infinite expression.

Each wave that emerges from the sea follows this golden mean spiral of proportional unity in relation to itself. The field of the heart also follows this precise proportional unity in relation to everything.

This is what WE are.

Love IS, and love spins in relation to . . . itself. Love IS and love spins in relation to . . . Everything!

Field 101, the Field of the Heart, and Coherency (Coherent-Sea) can be easily signaled through the symbol of the ocean. Let's play together as if we are at the beach to easily experience heart-centered awareness. We can choose to experience the field of the heart from the shoreline, or we may choose to swim in the sea of awareness, to float as one in the gentle currents of infinite potential. However we choose to experience our hearts, it can be as easy as a visit to the beach.

Breath of Possibility

Imagine now we are at the beach—any beach we choose. It is our private beach today. We get to play together without crowds. We may notice the ocean breeze blowing through our hair and the faint sound of the waves crashing on shore. We smell the sea air. We take a nice, deep breath now, and as we inhale, we fill our whole beings with the single breath of ALL interconnected life. As we exhale now, we allow our awareness to flow down into the center of our chests. This feels good, and so we do it again.

Breathe in Unity. Exhale Love. Drop awareness down into the center of your being. And again . . . Breathe in Possibility. Exhale Experience. Inhale Love. Exhale Love. We feel ourselves relax with each conscious breath we take. Our bodies soften. We soften in our awareness. We feel present. We feel expanded. We feel alive. We feel connected. We have just dropped into our hearts as easily as we breathe.

We are now drawn in awareness toward the ocean. We know exactly in which direction to move toward this sea of beauty; love as truth.

Barefoot in the Sand

As we step into the sand, we remove our shoes and go totally barefoot. We bare our soles to the softness of the Earth. We notice that each step we take on the silky sand leaves a unique footprint. No one else in the universe has that imprint of your foot, your unique sole signature. No one else in the universe has your unique spiritual soul signature either.

We walk together barefoot in the sand toward the not-so-distant ocean. As we move lightly and easily through the soft sand, we are invited to notice any thoughts, feelings, or sensations we are having as we connect to the beach, the emerging ocean, and the fresh air. Notice how, with every step, your feet seem to float, glide, and somehow fit perfectly into the sand no matter where you choose to step. You feel connected to the sand as though it were custom-made to comfort and conform to your feet.

This feeling of going barefoot in soft sand is a bit like dropping into the field of the heart in that we feel connected and comfortable. It feels easy. Soft. Natural. We feel connected to ourselves and connected to something bigger than ourselves, which, at some deeper implicate level, is still somehow us. As we move our awareness into our hearts, we may become aware of our bodies relaxing and even softening like the sand. Consider that going barefoot in the sand (or envisioning a bare-foot stroll in the sand) is an easy way to PLAY our way into our hearts. We drop into our hearts simply by choosing to notice the experience of connection.

As we are focusing on our feet creating imprints in the sand, we notice that the sand is becoming moist, as though water has woven itself between the granules. This new sensation draws our aware-ness immediately in front of us. We are at the shoreline where sand meets water. We are easily able to see the ocean spanning as far as the horizon in all directions from the point of our perspective on the sand. To our left and to our right, and in front of us, we notice the beauty of the sea. We are able to see the ripples of the sea expanding in all directions too. It seems that almost everywhere we look, there are ocean, waves, and endless ripples.

We are amid the ocean, symbol of the sea of infinite potential, a vast flow of limitless love and creative intelligence that we can choose to PLAY in from the field of the heart. We are witnessing love's reflection. We are witnessing our own boundless potential that is also found in the field of the heart.

Notice the sun's radiating brilliance upon the sea. Each wave is shimmering in its own magnificence. The sun and the sea are basking in their own reflection. Even when there are clouds, and storms, and even in darkness, the sun is always present for the sea, and the sea is always there for the sun. Love radiates. Love reflects. Love relates. Love elates in its own awareness.

As the ocean waves splash upon the shore, notice how the sand is shaped by this continual flow of the tides and currents. The gentle wind blows, and sand dunes ripple in a repetitive fractal fashion as far as you can see, in the same way the sea ripples endlessly. The field of the heart ripples this same way, in endless fractal fashion . . . and in endless fractal expansion.

Simply as easy as breathing, we are still in the field of the heart. We didn't think about it. We didn't worry about it. We didn't do anything.

We arrived by virtue of witnessing love's reflection. We are centered in our beings. We feel alive, connected, present, and expanded. We feel moved in our awareness by seeing beauty. We may feel a knowingness that transcends understanding. This knowing without knowing how we know is one way to recognize that we are in our hearts.

Perhaps we feel joyful for no apparent reason. This is the sheer Joy of Being. We are free to feel whatever we feel. Whatever we notice, feel, or experience, it's OK. Trust it. We may feel self-love. There may be an emerging form of self-awareness that is not a feeling of insecure self-consciousness but is an awareness of secure love in relation to self.

We are possibly tempted to ask if we are really in our hearts. As soon as we ask if we are in our hearts, our awareness may take us to our thoughts. So let's not wander there; rather, let's marvel in the wonder of knowing that the field of the heart is what we are. We are that. In the same way that the waves do not wonder whether they are ocean, we can relax in knowing that we are always the field of the heart. We are love. We are infinite potential. We are the field of the heart, and we can Trust our experience as we connect to this inner sea of love, power, and limitless creative intelligence.

To support our ease in accessing our heart fields, we may choose to center awareness in an external construct that represents the field of the heart. A fun way to do this is via something I call a Love Sphere. I often like to envision the heart field as being a spherical, transparent bubble of love surrounding me. Instead of dropping into my heart, I notice myself inside the center of a heart bubble, or Love Sphere, which represents the heart field. I might see this Love Sphere expanding several feet in all directions, or I might notice the Love Sphere expanding comfortably around me, its boundaries within reach of my physical body. Or I may stretch my arms and legs in all directions and still not touch the expansive boundary of this ever-present, omnipresent heart bubble of unconditional love. The boundaries of my Love Sphere can expand or constrict according to my awareness, preference, and choice in the moment. My awareness contains the field of the heart, yet the field of my heart is not contained by my awareness.

We may want to swim in the sea of love, in the sea of infinite potential, in the field of the heart. We can float in the sea while centered in our Love Spheres, if we choose.

Or we can choose another way. We may look down at the sand and notice two rafts shaped as inner tubes, one fluorescent green, the other bright yellow. We each choose one and move closer toward the water, leaving our Love Sphere at the shore.

In synchrony, we hoist our inner tubes above our heads and allow the inner tubes to drop down around the center of our chests. Our awareness follows this movement. Do this now. Drop the inner tube from above your head to your chest, or to wherever it feels comfortable. Do not worry about exact placement. Follow in your awareness as the tube drops from above your head down past your neck and even further down to the center of your body. Allow your arms to rest comfortably around the inner tube.

This inner tube represents the heart field. The field of the heart is not necessarily the physical heart or even the heart chakra. The field of the heart is a doughnut-shaped, counterrotating tube torus that resembles an inner tube. As a metaphorical construct, the inner tube can serve as a gauge to calibrate where we may be centering our awareness. However, the heart field includes all of us, as the field of the heart includes everything as part of itself. Even our feet are included in the heart field. Hence we can be in our hearts while we are aware of leaving footprints in the sand.

We gently take a few steps forward while staying in our hearts, and we enter into the water. Our inner tubes keep us buoyant. We float as, quickly, we lift our feet from the sand bar beneath us. We float as, quickly, we let go into the current and the ripples of the sea. As soon as now, we notice that all remaining sense of separation is replaced by awareness of flow. It is as though our bodies and minds have dissolved into the sea; in this merging, we cannot tell where we end and the ocean begins. We feel total peace.

This is truth as unity. From the field of the heart connected to the sea of infinite potential, we have access to all the possibility waves that are available in this vast ocean of our expanded awareness. Where do we want to focus? Which wave will we ride? What will we choose? For now, we are content simply Floating as One in the Ocean, One with All in the field of the heart. One with Field 101. One with Love. One. Just One.

$\mathcal{F}$102

Congruency. Compassion. Collaboration. Connection.

As we flow in the sea of infinite potential, accessible through the field of the heart, we have the power to choose where we want to resonate. We can choose which wave we want to ride, which field we want to play in. We can choose where we want to connect. Resonance is connection. Our resonance will determine which tide carries us, which current we will flow in that will create our momentum and experience. Field 102 supports us in connection, connection, connection.

Field 101 is the field of the heart and the sea of love and limitless potential, and Field 102 is congruent connection, being in community, reflected as collaboration, unified in completion. Field 102 supports us in connecting to any field in consciousness with ease and grace in flow.

MATT GIBSON/SHUTTERSTOCK

We are floating in the sea of infinite potential, centered in our Love Spheres, or we are buoyant in our inner tubes as an external representation of the field of the heart. From this space we have access to all. From this space we can connect to any field.

We look up to the sky and notice a group of starlings flying overhead. They are in a murmuration, where it seems hundreds of birds are flying together as one. They turn and flow together in synchrony, and to the observer, it is difficult to discern individual birds. New birds join the flock and, as if by magic, they are immediately synchronized to the entire flock or field of birds.

As we peacefully float in the sea of love, we also look down into the clear ocean and notice schools of fish swimming together in a harmony that cannot be explained by mere proximity. Even the most distant fish in the school is instantly aware of the movement of the fish in the center of the group and is swimming in synchrony with fish on the opposite side of the school. It is as if there is no distance because they are all in flowing movement as one.

RICH CAREY/SHUTTERSTOCK

Connection to Field 102 can be easily signaled by the symbol of a flock of birds flying in flow or a school of fish swimming in synchrony. The symbol of Birds or Fish in synchronized flowing movement can serve to represent your conscious connection to Field 102. As we connect, so we experience.

Consider now a new Field you would like to connect to in order to experience something new and different in your love hologram. You can leverage Field 102 to activate the field flow of that chosen Field.

Center in your Love Sphere, the field of your heart, or the inner tube construct to support heart-centered awareness. Feel free to signal Field 101 for heart-centered awareness, if you choose.

Now, with intent to connect to Field 102, leverage the symbol of a flock of birds or a school of fish to experience Field 102 connection. Feel into the field experience as though you are watching the movement of a Field in form and action. While remaining aware of that connection, allow for Field 102 to support you in connecting to your Field of choice.

19

What do you notice as you connect to Field 102 and this new Field of choice? What perceptions, feelings, sensations, thoughts, or experiences come into your awareness? Write this down if you choose. How might this connection to your chosen field influence your experiences? Pay attention. Remain present in your connection to this chosen Field of choice by virtue of your established connection through Field 102. Allow for your awareness to congruently remain aligned with this Field while staying in a state of coherency in your heart. Coherency from your heart while congruently aligning awareness with a field of choice will signal a field flow that will express in your love hologram. Take notes as reciprocal signals of intent are returned based on your chosen Field. Remember that a signal of intent will activate the corresponding symmetric wave of any chosen field. You will never activate a field flow that does not correspond to your intent. Field 102 will connect you to any field, anywhere, at any time.

$\mathcal{F}$103

Neutrality. Release Judgments and Attachments.

We are centered in the field of our hearts, in our Love Spheres, and have activated the process of choosing where we want to resonate in a sea of limitless potential. As we are playing in a new, more liberating way to create in our love holograms, it is important to remain neutral about our experiences and manifestations and not to judge ourselves, or others.

While our hearts are neutral, our thoughts and emotions may have charges that keep us bound to a polarized state of mind. Field 103 supports us in the art and science of neutrality and in living devoid of judgments.

Our judgments about ourselves, others, and the way we "think" reality should be are limited observations that weigh us down, like heavy anchors preventing movement in our awareness, stifling the flow of new experiences. Judgments create rip tides of no change. Judgments siphon off components of the sea of love as limitless potential and trap potential power and possibilities in the vortex of our limiting perceptions.

Field 103 supports us in being free from judgment. We are able to access neutrality and can thus create new trails in our reality in our love holograms.

Additionally, Field 103 supports us in being neutral, where we may notice no charge for or against something needing to be a certain way. Field 103 allows for us to flow with presence in the moment. This is a gift of grace.

To signal Field 103, we may leverage the symbol of the nautilus shell. The nautilus shell is a popular representation of the golden mean, a spiral of love reflecting proportional unity and symmetry in relation to itself, leveraging the asymmetry of Fibonacci's sequence.

The main feature of the nautilus is its large, snail-like shell that is coiled upward and lined with mother-of-pearl. The shell is subdivided into as many as thirty chambers. As the shell grows, the empty chambers are used to regulate buoyancy. A cross section of the shell of the nautilus will show the cycles of its growth as a series of chambers arranged in a precise golden mean spiral.

The functional utility of the nautilus shell is its ability to adjust buoyancy in relation to changing currents in the ocean. This reflects a creative intel-

EUGENE SIM/SHUTTERSTOCK

EUGENE SIM/SHUTTERSTOCK

ligence that we will leverage to support resonance with neutrality as we engage in the art of interactive reality creation.

The nautilus shell is the home of the chambered nautilus in the vast ocean where this creature flows. Interestingly, the structure of this multichambered shell does not weigh the nautilus down but is actually a buoyancy compensator. The chambered nautilus uses this structure to maintain *neutral buoyancy*. The shell is how this conscious creature accesses neutrality in a dynamic sea of change—by filling the inner chambers with a formulation that provides for neutral buoyancy.

The nautilus shell is a symbol for neutrality rendered in the proportions of symmetry with asymmetry—perfectly imperfect physics, the physics of love. We will utilize this intelligent structure to support our resonance with the Field of Neutrality. The nautilus shell is our chosen symbol for Field 103. (You may choose something different, if that is your preference.)

Drop down into your heart and simply Be. Center in your Love Sphere, if you choose, or in your inner tube construct for heart-centered aware-ness, if that is your preference. You may signal Field 101 for support. From this space of heart-centered awareness and coherency, consider something in your life you want to change. It may be a situation, a relationship, or even a global pattern.

Allow for any symbol, color, or object to come into your awareness that represents this patterned perception you want to change. See this symbol floating in your awareness, either outside your Love Sphere or beyond your inner tube. Notice where the symbol is positioned in relation to you; is the symbol directly in front of you, off to the left, or somewhere behind you? Pay attention to where this symbol is positioned without judgment or second-guessing.

Now, while remaining in the field of the heart, designate a position that represents Field 103, Neutrality, and allow for the image of the nautilus shell to appear floating in that chosen space. What-ever feels right to you, trust that. It matters less where you choose to position the nautilus shell than it does that you choose. Just choose.

Simply notice where the nautilus shell is positioned relative to the symbol that represents what you want to change. Recognizing that the nautilus shell is able to create neutral buoyancy in the sea of love as limitless potential, allow for your awareness to gently move the symbol you want to change inside the nautilus shell.

As the pattern you want to change is integrated with the neutral buoyancy of the nautilus shell, what perceptions, feelings, sensations, thoughts, or experiences come into your awareness? Write these down, if you choose.

When this integration is complete and the symbol you want to change is nested inside the nautilus shell, pay close attention to what the nautilus shell does naturally. Does the shell stay in the same position? If so, let it be.

Does it sink down in your awareness or move away from or above you? If so, this symbolically means that the nautilus shell needs to recalibrate itself for neutrality in relation to this new occupant/pattern of consciousness. To remove any positive or negative charge affecting the buoyant neutrality of the nautilus shell, from the field of your heart (signaling 101 for assistance, as needed), see a stream of white light-love filling the chambers of the nautilus shell where the symbol you want to change is occupied. Continue beaming the light of love until the nautilus moves to the position you previously designated as neutrality.

When in this neutral position, what do you notice about the pattern that you previously wanted to change? What perceptions, feelings, sensations, thoughts, or experiences come into your awareness? Write these down, if you choose.

How might this connection to Field 103, Neutrality, through the symbol of the nautilus shell, influence how you relate to this pattern? How does being neutral feel to you? How might neutrality through Field 103 favorably influence other experiences in your love hologram? Leverage the nautilus shell and Field 103 anytime you sense that you are going into judgment or need freedom from charges for or against a pattern. Neutrality is a freedom to flow with change in the interest of love.

F104

Containers. Creation. Reality Structuring for Manifestation.

Field 104 is a field of spiraling torsion fields that nest together to form matter and experience. The nesting of the torsion fields, which carry information, is what allows geometries of love to reflect in our love holograms. These geometries may be physical structures, or they may be resonant experiences. Though this is a field of spirals, voluminous with potential, it can be useful to create grids or templates through which we may organize our spiraling manifestations in process. Thus, again, we turn to nature to determine an efficient way to leverage Field 104 and map what works for universal creative intelligence so it may also work for us.

We will continue our focus on being and living from the field of the heart in all endeavors, but we shall now begin doing so in the spirit of BEE-ing: BEE-ing as in honeybees.

Honeycomb Hexagons

Have you ever wondered why honeybees build hexagonal patterns in the wax combs of their hives?

The reason, proved by Thomas Hales in 1999 in what is called the "honeycomb conjecture," is that the hexagonal structure with its six sides is the most efficient and compact of any of the geometric patterns available to the bees. Not all bees use this structure. However, because the hexagon is the structure that permits for the most efficient packing, storing, and retrieving of large amounts of information in three dimensions, we will follow the wise lead of the honeybee for manifesting True Authentic Desires (TADs), the honey of our hearts, in our love holograms.

Hexagons in Science

Scientists are also now looking into the hexagonal structure of graphene as a form of free energy, given its incredible electrical conductivity and amazing energy-transferring ability. Graphene is the thinnest material known to mainstream scientists. Even though graphene is super thin, as a material, it is phenomenally strong. Graphene is also very flexible. Because of its flexibility, it can

ANDREY_KUZMIN/SHUTTERSTOCK

be twisted and curved to a certain extent without breaking.

What is fascinating to me about the hexagon is that if it is twisted 180 degrees and the ends are connected, the hexagon forms a tube torus (doughnut) resembling our heart fields. Thus the hexagon seems an ideal structure through which to pack one-dimensional formless information into two-dimensional structure to create three-dimensional matters and experiences. The hexagon honeycomb lattice structure is our chosen symbol for Field 104. (You may choose something different, if that is your preference.)

Center now in your Love Sphere. Signal Field 101 to access heart-centered awareness to assist you, if you choose. Now, consider something you genuinely want to manifest. It may be an experience, a relationship, a new job, a new house, or anything that you may Truly Authentically Desire. Signal Field 104 for reality structuring. From the field of the heart, coupled with your mind's eye, project another Love Sphere in front of you. This second Love Sphere can be any size you choose, and you may modify the size any time you want to fit your manifestations in progress.

In the spirit of honeybees, allow for a six-sided hexagon to appear in the Love Sphere in front of you. The hexagon may be any size you choose. Now, connected to the desired manifestation (leveraging Field 102, if you choose), see the desired manifestation as a word or object, and insert the word or object into the hexagon inside your Love Sphere in front of you.

Create three additional hexagons that are connected to the original hexagon. From the field of the heart, what additional informational ingredients are needed to manifest this True Authentic Desire? Consider three key components, and place each one in its own respective hexagon connected to the object of chosen manifestation. Excellent!

Consider whether there are more than three key components needed for this manifestation. If so, feel free to add as many connected hexagons and to fill them with the information or ideas that occur to you.

As soon as you feel that you have filled the Love Sphere with all the spiraling potentialities needed, interconnected efficiently for the exchange of information through each hexagon, allow yourself to feel into this manifestation as though it already is.

What do you notice? What perceptions, feelings, sensations, thoughts, or experiences come into your awareness as you connect to this manifestation as though it IS already happening and available in your love hologram? Write these down, if you choose. The manifestation process has already begun. It shall continue through our conscious connection to additional fields that support us in manifestation.

𝓕105

Receivership. Intuition. Listening. Development of Manifestation.

Field 105 is conducive to manifesting True Authentic Desires, as it supports us in receivership, intuition, and listening, key facets of interactive reality creation in our Love Spheres. This field has overtones of the sacred feminine essence characterized by intuition, inclusion, receivership, and community.

To support us in consciously connecting to Field 105, we again turn to the secret, magical world of honeybees. The honeybee (and bees in general) have been a symbol of the divine feminine since time immemorial. The honeybee itself relies on its intuitive knowingness, an internal GPS that tells the bee where to go or what needs to be done next. These amazing creatures venture from their hives, journeying to collect food for the

RTBILDER/SHUTTERSTOCK

whole—the collective group. All bee colonies work together and follow their inborn intuitive guidance systems.

Every bee has its own specific job function, and that job does not interfere with any of the other bees. Every bee is important and fulfills its individual role to the best of its ability. Bees are highly intuitive creatures that fulfill their life purpose as all for one and one for all.

The honeybee is our chosen symbol to signal Field 105 so that we may access intuition more consistently. (You may choose something different, if that is your preference.) Like a honeybee, we may be easily fine-tuned for receivership of inherent intuitive knowing. Field 105 supports resonant recognition of intuition any time we choose.

To me, intuition is "knowing without knowing how we know." It is an inner accurate sense that is beyond the standard senses of tangible awareness. We may not be able to see the information, or smell it, or taste it, or touch it, or hear it, but we have an awareness that directs our knowing—a knowing what to do, where to go, when to do it, and often even how to do it. We seem always to know, in the same way a GPS system can always direct us to a desired destination. The GPS functions based on satellite signaling. When we tune in to our Intuition Satellite, listen and receive and trust the messages we receive, when we follow our intuition as an Inner Global Positioning System connected to everything, in the same way we follow a GPS in a car, we are rarely led astray.

A delightful side effect of heart-centered awareness is increased intuitive ability. Trusting the gut, our intuitive hunches, can serve us in consistently loving and living extraordinary lives. Intuition is based on far more information than the logical mind can access. We can trust our intuition. Field 105 supports us in all that we may choose to intuit, receive, and ultimately experience in our love holograms.

Drop down into the field of the heart. Center in your Love Sphere, if you choose, and signal Field 101 for support, as needed. Now signal Field 105. You may choose to signal it simply for more intuitive guidance. Alternatively, you may want to signal Field 105 to receive information pertaining to a creative manifestation process begun in the prior Practical Play with Field 104.

However you choose to connect to Field 105, leverage the honeybee as a symbol of intuitive knowing, receivership, and a sense of knowing what to do and when to do it.

If relating this exercise to the prior manifestation exercise, ask yourself what additional information you need to intuit, receive, and then add to the hexagon template already created. Add whatever occurs to you now or at a later time.

If you were to know what do and when to do it, like a honeybee, what would occur to you in this moment? Write that down, if you choose. How does connecting to Field 105, and the intuitive realm of honeybees, a symbol of sacred feminine intuition and communal connection, support you in manifesting True Authentic Desires?

Invite the symbol of the honeybee to go out and gather any information needed in the same way the bees gather food for the hive. Remember to store whatever intuitive information the bees bring back to you in the hexagonal lattice of your Love Sphere.

Notice what else remains to do, from a space of being in the field of the heart. Consider taking action like a bee preparing a hive. Where may you need to pollinate thoughts, ideas, and actions in your love hologram? Leverage Field 105 for support in this creative process. We shall soon discover another Field instrumental to delivering our manifestations as actualizations in our love holograms.

F106

Action. Abundance. Delivery of Manifestation.

This field is powered by the abundance of the universe coupled with the will to act as the expression of limitless potential in all ways. Field 106 supports birthing new loving experiences for self and others as a reflection of the infinite.

A key principle in the manifestation process is allowance as a function of flow. In the same way a baby is generally not delivered before it is ready, in the same way a flower does not blossom before its time, mastering manifestation means recognizing that the process has its own rhythm that follows the natural order of the universe. This is allowing, not pushing.

Whereas time may only be a construct of consciousness, timing as rhythmic flow is a function of universal connection to creative intel-

ALEKSANDAR MIJATOVIC/SHUTTERSTOCK

ligence. Field 106 supports our movement of awareness from the womb of creation to actual experience in flow. Field 106 supports the blossoming of
our manifestations into three-dimensional reality.

Our symbol for connecting to Field 106 is the
sunflower in full bloom. An open sunflower is a
symbol of abundance as well as joy, sustenance,
and happiness. Delivering abundant new joyful
creations is precisely what resonance with Field
106 supports in our love holograms.

Sunflowers are heliotropic, which means they
turn their heads to the sun. Although the exact
reason for this behavior is not confirmed, some
speculate that this happens when sunflowers are
ready to receive pollination from bees. They turn
and face the light when they are ready to be in
receivership.

We receive and deliver when we are ready. In
an abundant universe, all is available. In an abundant universe, opening to that abundance, like
a sunflower opening, blossoming, and turning
toward the light, will signal pollinating our desires
as actual manifested experiences.

GORNJAK/SHUTTERSTOCK

There is a popular anonymous quote that says, "When the flower blossoms the bee will come." This essentially means that the flower doesn't wait for the bee to Open. Field 106 is about opening to abundance Now. Do not wait for the bee. Do not wait for the hexagon hive to be built. Do not wait for anything. Open Now to abundance.

Allow for abundance to blossom in all that you relate to, including the desired manifestations. Cultivate an abundance of appreciation for all that you have already manifested in your life. Like a sunflower, blossom now and appreciate the sunshine reflected in all your experiences. The more we resonate in a field of abundance, the more abundance resonates with us.

Flow-er of Abundance: Field 106 supports us in the full recognition that abundance is a state of being characterized by unity, flow, joy, and appreciation. Flow as abundance. As the flow-er in this field, abundance will follow.

Abundance is a resonant field that lacks nothing. It is resonate with abundance, and abundance flows into all that we are and all that we do. Abundance is the dance of universal consciousness and its infinite potential expressing itself in limitless ways. The more we resonate with the field of abundance, the more we may notice and experience abundance in all endeavors.

Drop into the field of the heart and center in your Love Sphere. Signal Field 101 to support you, if you choose. Signal your intent to connect to Field 106, Abundance, with Flow. Leverage the fully blossomed sunflower as an image to activate your resonant awareness of Field 106 as Abundance, and simply Open. Open your awareness to the abundance of the universe, of your creative potential and your ability to manifest experiences that reflect the symmetry of abundance in your love hologram.

Abundance is amplified when we are cultivating a sense of appreciation. Where in your life now can you cultivate more appreciation? Abundantly appreciate what is working in your life. Abundantly appreciate the simple things. Sunshine. Water. Food. Friendship. Free time. Even appreciate your bills, for they represent an abundance of services that you have already received.

As this Field also supports timing of delivery of desired manifestations, we can leverage this connection to complete the manifestation process we may have begun with Field 104 and Field 105 in previous Practical Plays.

Know that the honeycomb, the honeybee, and the sunflower are all mutually dependent upon one other for the completion of the manifestation process. Similarly, Fields 104–106 work symbiotically and synergistically in supporting the manifestation process. We do not necessarily need to work with each one in successive order. In the same way that the flower does not wait for the bee to blossom, the order in which we activate our connection to these Fields matters not. In fact, we may find that we are drawn to connect with all of them simultaneously or with one at a time in a random order. Trust whatever occurs for you in the moment. Stay present and follow where your awareness goes. If ever you feel you do not know, like a sunflower, turn to the light and be guided intuitively to create, receive, and deliver True Authentic Desires into manifested experiences. In-Joy!

$\mathcal{F}$107

Clarity. Clear Confusion and Fear Programs.

Penny for Our Thoughts of Clarity

What may stop us from noticing that we are in our hearts and experiencing the power of heart-centered awareness are limiting thoughts. Limiting thoughts that occur in repetition become memetic (viral) and can function like recurring programs in our love holograms. These habitual programs keep us in resonance with larger, more powerful morphic fields of limitation. Field 107 is a clearing Field that provides for clarity in relation to . . . everything!

Some offer a penny for our thoughts. We choose to access the eternal treasure in our hearts.

Take a moment and allow for the image of a penny to form and float a few inches above your head. Position the coin on its edge so you cannot see whether it is facing heads or tails. Both sides are of the same coin, and the penny is only whole when both sides (heads and tails) are included as part of itself. We are the same. We are only able to recognize our wholeness when we integrate our polarities from the field of the heart. The field of the heart is unity, from which all duality expresses. The field of the heart is the whole coin, albeit with infinite value.

Now imagine that there is a coin slot in the center of the top of your head, similar to a coin slot found at the top of a piggy bank.

Leveraging your awareness, drop the penny into the slot and allow the penny to drop down through your head now. Follow your awareness as the penny continues to drop down through your neck and down into the center of your chest, into a pool of water that represents the field of the heart.

If you want to, you can let the penny drop all the way to your belly button before it hits the surface of the pool. Be surprised where the penny natu-rally makes its splash. As the penny moves down through your body, allow your awareness to move with the penny as though your awareness and the penny were one. One cent. One sense. One inner sense of unity. Allow for the penny and your aware-ness to drop into the water as if the water were the center and the whole of your being simultane-ously. You are in the field of your heart. You are in the flow of being as water.

Notice the ripples in the water as the penny merges with the pool. Notice how the ripples move out in concentric flow. As you follow the ripples with your awareness, maintain connection to them and experience them as though they were you. Experience the ripples as you, because they are you. These ripples are the waves of interconnection between one sense and all senses. Between you and All that you are in relation to. Between you and All That is. There is no separation between the field of the heart and you, and all that you relate to in your love hologram.

What do you notice as your awareness drops from your head into your heart? Do you feel centered, expanded, present, peaceful, joyful, tearful, grateful? Do you feel a softening? Do you feel nothing? Whatever you notice is perfect.

Sometimes we feel nothing initially when dropping awareness into the heart. This is because we are connecting to potential before it is expression. We are connecting to a preconditioned essence as unconditional love. No conditions means no thoughts or emotions. Yet we can notice the experience of being in the field of the heart through our sensory nervous system. We may feel calm, peaceful, present, and clear. We may feel Open. Simply Open.

From Cloudy to Clarity, and the Sky Is Not the Limit

Now even though we are in the field of the heart, we may still be having thoughts. A key is to not let our thoughts have us. Our limiting thoughts are akin to clouds in the sky that shield us from experiencing sunshine and clear views of infinite possibilities. If we attach our awareness to the clouds as though we are the clouds, as though we are the thoughts, then that is all we may experience. However, if we expand our awareness and notice our thoughts simply as clouds floating by in the sky, a small part of much bigger scenery, then we are able to have thoughts as part of our experience, but the thoughts do not define or limit the experience.

Thoughts are like clouds as they can shape the skyline (or parameters) of our love holograms. However, thoughts do not define or limit the skyline, for the sky has no limits. Neither do WE!

As we are centered in the field of the heart, we may want to leverage Field 107 to clear recurring thought patterns and their corresponding limiting fields. For example, we may be afraid to take the next step in our business, and so we keep thinking, "I am not ready." This thought and its associated fear signal larger global fields of fear, insufficiency, and stagnation. Although none of these memes and corresponding fields are necessarily true about us, when we are in resonance with these thought fields, our experiences play out accordingly in limited manners.

Rather than seeing ourselves clearly, we are cloudy in confusion. Field 107 can be signaled by the symbol of clouds in the sky being swept away by the wind, as a loving cloud-sweeper. Clouds of confusion are replaced by blue skies, clarity, unity, and love.

As you drop into the field of the heart, consider something you are struggling with in your love hologram. Whatever occurs to you, write it down, if you choose. Consider what limiting thoughts or fields you may be in resonance with that are perpetuating this sense of struggle.

For every limiting thought or limiting field that occurs to you, identify that thought or field as a cloud in the skyline of your love hologram. Allow for many thoughts or fields of confusion to come into your sky as clouds. When you feel complete for now (and you can repeat this as necessary, anytime), take a moment and observe the sky. How cloudy is it? Can you even see the skyline, or do you see one continuous cloud? Note your answer, and allow yourself to see love's humor in the clouds. What an interesting creation. No judgment. Simply clouds.

Now signal intent to connect to Field 107 and see the Field symbolically as a loving cloud-blower. It may be a blowing wind or a tree leaf blower or whatever occurs to you. For me, Field 107 is represented by the image of the continual movement of clouds across a blue sky. For you, it may be represented by something different, and that is perfect.

See Field 107 coming in and blowing the clouds away. Notice that only the cloudy thoughts of confusion are blown away. Clear thoughts remain as transparent as the blue sky. As each thought of limitation flows off into the distance, as each field of limitation is no longer in your resonant awareness, what do you notice?

How does experiencing clarity about the truth of who you are, and what you are capable of creating and experiencing, seem to change up configurations in your love hologram? How does access to this Field enable you to relate to your thoughts differently? How are you empowered to relate to yourself and others in more liberating ways?

An alternate way to play with this Field is to explore the clouds with curiosity. Rather than leveraging Field 107 to blow these thoughts out of your love hologram, you may choose to enter into the clouds with Field 107 and ask them to tell you what you have yet to recognize about yourself. Realize that all limitations are simply programs of confusion. Perhaps these thoughts continue to occur as placeholders beckoning our attention, recognition, and love. Sending love to the thoughts through connection to Field 107 will allow the clouds to go POOF, like magic. So Field 107 is a cloud-poofer, too, if we choose.

POOF! Limitations can evaporate with love.

Lastly, remember that limiting thoughts and corresponding fields are not necessarily a detriment. They are simply a part of our experience; they do not define us, or our experiences.

Limitations, like clouds, can create textures and distinctions in our scenery, in our love holograms. As long as we allow these clouds to be and to pass,

SUEC/SHUTTERSTOCK

the experience of the thoughts and their corresponding fields will be and will pass too. Clear skies ahead. Clear skies Now!

Signal Field 107 any time you want to change the weather in your love hologram. Whether you know or don't know what is causing the confusion, Field 107 will support clarity as the Clear-ALL field of love.

F108

Perfectly Imperfect. True Authentic Self (TAS).

Field 108 is a Field of being perfectly imperfect. We are already complete AND we are a continual work in progress as we rediscover, remember, and reclaim this truth. We are both limitless potential and perceived limitation as one.

The True Authentic Self embodies limitlessness with limitations. Our TAS has awareness of our core essence as a limitless being, our True Self, which is unconditional love as coherent light. TAS also has limiting self-concepts (Authentic Self) that have been conditioned into personal awareness. These coexist and synthesize as one, without judgment. Our TAS knows that perceived limitations are still inherently connected to that which is limitless love.

Authenticity is the epitome of embodying our True Authentic Self (TAS). The True Authentic Self embodies limitlessness with limitations. In effect, it says, "I know I am consciousness potential and a being without limits, and yet I coexist peacefully with my self-imposed limitations. Daily, in each moment, I am unfolding and letting go of who I was the moment before so that I can embrace more of who I am becoming."

Our TAS is "perfectly imperfect."

Field 108 supports the full recognition of integrity as completion with TAS and all that we relate to in our lives. It is not our limitations that cause us strife. Rather, it is how we may relate to our limitations that prevents us from experiencing joy, flow, and self-love. This field supports us in relating to our perceived limitations with integrity as wholeness, self-love, patience, forgiveness, and self-acceptance.

You Are the Symbol

Connecting to Field 108 is truly a unique experience. For this reason, there is no symbol to represent our connection to this Field of Authenticity. WE are the symbol. You are the symbol. There is nothing in this universe that can represent True Authentic Self (TAS) better than you. You are a unique expression of universal consciousness experiencing individuality, and no one else can symbolize and reflect this essential truth better than you. Embrace and embody the Field of TAS through your own reflection.

Sure, there may be symbols in nature that remind you of aspects of your TAS. If you would like to assign a symbol as your own unique code to signal Field 108, please feel free to do so. Just choose. Yet if you find that in a few days, months, or years, you no longer relate to that chosen symbol in the same way you have related to it in the past, please choose anew.

Remember, daily we are evolving into more of whom we truly are. In each moment, we shed layers of ourselves that no longer fit us, like outgrown shoes. Integration of our sense of limitation with our limitless nature enables us to freely adorn new ways of being and relating that always feel like going barefoot in the sand. We are comfortable in being who we truly are. We are comfortable in our own skin, in our own truth as integrity.

So choose an object that may remind you of your TAS. Or, look in the mirror now and say hello to you, a perfectly imperfect reflection of Field 108. Let You be the signal for Field 108. Let your authenticity, integrity, self-love, and self-acceptance be the beacon for this field of freedom, congruency, and individuality. You are perfectly imperfect. We are perfectly imperfect.

Drop down into the field of the heart. Center in your Love Sphere. Signal Field 101 if you choose. Now, with intent to connect to Field 108, see your-self as the symbol for this Field. What does it feel like now to allow yourself to integrate the parts of yourself you may not like with the parts of yourself

IZO/SHUTTERSTOCK

you may appreciate? Feel this answer now as an authentic experience. How does accepting yourself exactly as you are in this moment, perfectly imperfect, allow you freedom to be seen transparently by self and by others? How does this acceptance and integration further free you to change, if you choose?

Any time we disallow or disavow aspects of ourselves that we judge, we siphon off potential power and potential love. Embrace the yucky stuff, integrate, and allow for the light of love to transform the patterns in your awareness.

How does this allowance of All of you open you to experiencing more flow, more joy, more love, and more personal power? How does integrating limitless love with all that may appear otherwise enable you to live in your heart and relate to yourself with compassion and honesty? Take note of these answers, and pay particularly close attention to the answers that feel uncomfortable. That may be a sign to bring more awareness, acceptance, love, and possibility into the answer. Embrace being exactly who you are, and discover the Joy

WIKTORIA PAWLAK/SHUTTERSTOCK

of Being TAS, for living and loving our perfectly imperfect selves is simply fanTAStic!

F109

Access to Joy.

Field 109 is simply a Field of joy. Joy is our natural state when we stop being everything we are not. Joy is a facet of heart-centered awareness. Joy is a facet of being our True Authentic Self (TAS). Joy is always available to us, if we choose.

Just like sunshine is not ever really gone on a cloudy day, joy is not really ever gone but is merely obscured by our clouds as confusion surrounding circumstances. Our joy is never gone. We may choose to rediscover our joy, and this realization is key to finding it. Just choose.

Field 109 facilitates resonance with joy regardless of what has happened, is happening, or may happen. Joy Is as Love Is and is always available if we open to it.

BAJINDA/SHUTTERSTOCK

How do we rediscover joy? We open to it and make ourselves available to this Field resonance. Field 109 is here to support us.

Our chosen symbol for Field 109 is a ladybug. You may choose something different, if that is your preference. Many consider a ladybug to be a symbol of good luck and what good luck we have to rediscover our joy. Luck is resonance, and resonance with a Field of joy will bring forth the abundance of the universe.

A ladybug is a little magical creature that brings wonder and delight to the hearts of young children. We are reminded of our joy when we watch children playing with and experiencing ladybugs. Ladybugs remind us to become like little children and remember the magic of our existence. This, too, brings forth joy from within our hearts. Embracing our hearts like little children who are open and filled with love can support us in experiencing our joy.

Ladybugs are simple joy. They are content in their beingness, with or without spots, no matter their color. They are seemingly content wherever they may be. Ladybugs are signs of abundance, and an abundance of joy is our natural state. Experience the Joy of Being through Field 109.

Ladybugs are harmless to humans. They may remind us to stop harming ourselves, which enables us to access more joy. Though small in size, the ladybug is fearless. As fear cannot exist in the presence of joy, the ladybug reminds us to get back in touch with the joy of living.

When we allow for joy in our lives, our fears take a backseat. We are no longer driven by what we want to avoid but rather are driven by the vehicle and volition of joy.

How do we rediscover our joy? First, we remember that it is never truly gone. It may be buried or obstructed, but it is always present. Joy lives eternally in our hearts.

So let's drop into our hearts now and center in our Love Spheres, if we choose. Signal 101 for assistance, as needed. Now invite Field 109, Joy, into our awareness.

Allow for this Field of joy to tickle you like a ladybug might as it gently lands on your open hand. Notice that if you close your hand, the ladybug will be trapped and smothered. Joy is this way too. Joy relies on us to keep an open hand and open heart. Joy seeks to flow freely and to flutter toward wherever there is an opening or an invitation. Open to Joy. Invite joy as Field 109 to play. Open to the heart of You.

Joy cannot be contained once it is recognized, released, and experienced.

Like a ladybug, joy has no plan other than what appears in the moment.

Ask yourself, if you knew what brought you joy from within, what thoughts, ideas, sensations, or experiences would come to your awareness? Perhaps it is a walk on the beach, playing the guitar, dancing, or reading a delicious novel by a warm fire on a cold winter's night. Connect to that feeling now, and allow for it to expand into all of your body, mind, and being. Now, if you were to allow that feeling of joy to be present with you no matter what you may be doing, how might that change your experiences and all that you relate to? Write down what you discover, if you choose.

Joy is not situational, and yet joy can be found and experienced in situations. We are wise to acknowledge these joy-filled moments when they occur, for they are placeholders reflecting our heart's true essence. Joy. Love. Flow. Connection.

Contrary to most perceptions, joy is not a life of bliss. Joy is a reflection of authenticity, connection to personal truth, and a knowing that we are part of something that is bigger than that which is ourselves.

Joy is being true to the currents that move us always from the river of forgetting toward the sea of remembering: love, unity, and limitless potential. Joy is being true to you as love's reflection.

Experience the Joy of Being like a ladybug, and flutter with a heart of joy as you choose.

F110

True Authentic Power (TAP). Fluid Boundaries.

Field 110 provides strength and assertion in standing up for yourself in relation to what is right, true, and correct in the moment authentically, as we make choices. This Field supports our ability to listen to our hearts and make choices based on inner knowing, trust, integrity, and what brings us joy.

Field 110 also gives easy access to True Authentic Power based on inner knowing, as cultivated by heart-centered awareness and clarity of mind. This is heart–mind synthesis characterized by stability with flow.

Choice with discernment is a facet of Fluid Boundaries. Fluid Boundaries are boundaries that aren't predefined in anticipation of situations or experiences. We flow in the moment as a movement from within our hearts. If you have never been very adept at practicing Fluid Bound-

LEUNGCHOPAN/SHUTTERSTOCK

aries, this does not mean you cannot master this in the moment and with conscious practice by connecting to Field 110.

This Field enables us to make choices from our hearts that are congruently aligned with self-love, honor, dignity, integrity, and personal truth. Furthermore, this Field supports us in going with the flow such that we do not betray ourselves to circumstances.

We may bend with the winds of changing circumstances, but we are never broken. The symbol for this Field is the Chinese bamboo tree, a tree that bends and yet is able to remain stable and sturdy amid life's storms. (You may choose something else, if you prefer.)

Part of bamboo's strength lies in its complex root foundation. The bamboo has such resilience as it is truly firmly connected to itself and to its soil such that it is able to withstand even the harshest of circumstances. These roots do not hold the bamboo back; rather, they serve as a firm foundation for integrity, self-respect, and choice with discernment.

This remarkable tree is different from most trees in that it doesn't grow in the usual fashion. Whereas most trees grow steadily over a period of years, the Chinese bamboo tree doesn't break through the ground for the first four years. Then, in the fifth year, the tree begins to grow at an astonishing rate. This tree can grow up to ninety feet in five weeks! So, like bamboo, we can grow quickly in our practice of Fluid Boundaries.

Field 110 also supports our ability to take action and move forward. This action of *doing* is from a space of heart-centered *being*. Like the Chinese bamboo that appears to be doing nothing for the first four years of its life, and suddenly grows and flourishes, Field 110 will support the action necessary for growth, expansion, and blossoming following cultivation, planning, and preparing. Action is necessary for creative intelligence to fulfill its own potential. Take action with the support of Field 110. Be like bamboo: strong and sturdy, resilient, and able to grow by leaps and bounds when you are ready.

Drop down into the field of the heart and center in your Love Sphere, if you choose. Signal intent to connect to Field 110. You may see an image of a bamboo tree to support your resonant recognition of this Field connection.

Now consider a situation where you are unable to maintain respectful boundaries for yourself with others. Feel into the situation, and notice how it makes you feel. If you were able to exhibit Fluid

Boundaries, bending with flow to the circumstances without compromising your integrity, how might you relate differently? What would it feel like to respond in the moment with flow to what you truly want in the situation, without being pushed around by others? Write down any thoughts, feelings, sensations, or experiences that occur for you now. How does access to Fluid Boundaries through Field 110 change up how you relate to most circumstances in your love hologram?

Now, consider a scenario where you have not taken the action necessary to complete a project or to attain closure in a circumstance. Connect to the Chinese bamboo tree and realize that, like this special tree, action has been occurring under the surface. With the support of Field 110, notice all the intricate distinctions that have been made relative to this chosen project or circumstance that is still pending. Action has been taken. You are not stuck. You are never stuck in the same way the Chinese bamboo tree is never idle in the first four years of its life.

If you were to become more aware of the actions you have already taken, how could that awareness support you in moving to the surface where the roots can take shape as a growing plant? What specific choices can you make now (choice with discernment) to support action moving forward toward completion? What steps can you take toward closure? Write these down, if you choose.

Remember, Field 110 is doing from a state of being in heart-centered awareness. Stay connected to your heart as you choose wisely. Notice that soon, as now, like the bamboo tree, you have laid a firm foundation in integrity and that your growth in expressing Fluid Boundaries, choice with discernment, and taking action is exponential.

$F111$

Divine Alignment Synchronicity.

This Field supports our ability to recognize divine alignment as it is occurring in our love holograms. There are as many ways to recognize divine alignment as there are expressions of infinite potential.

Field 111 facilitates greater awareness of synchronicity. *Synchronicity*, a term coined by Carl Jung, "is the coming together of inner and outer events in a way that cannot be explained by cause and effect and that is meaningful to the observer."

Thus synchronicity is noticing the interconnected patterns of everything and recognizing that there is no such thing as coincidence. Although we may be the meaning-makers of our experiences, taking note of synchronicities when they occur can facilitate greater awareness of our connection to all that is possible and available in our love holograms. Field 111 supports us in recognizing these forms of divine alignments.

A very common and easy way to play with this Field of divine alignment is through our relationship to numbers. As placeholders in our awareness, numbers appearing in our awareness in meaningful configurations can serve to support us in realizing that we are in flow and that all is in order, despite circumstances that may appear otherwise.

These meaningful coincidences with numbers are a form of synchronicity, a divine alignment reminding us of the intricate interconnectedness of our holographic reality.

We may be making a key decision and look at the clock, only to notice it says 11:11. All is aligned, and this placeholder in our awareness serves as a momentary reassurance that all is in order. Perhaps you are looking for a new job and the interview is held in suite 222 of a building you have never visited. Or maybe you have written a book and the section about synchronicity randomly appears exactly on page 111 in the final print edition.

One of my favorite ways to leverage Field 111 is by noticing how all the fields show up in my awareness through numbers. I may be taking an airplane flight assigned Flight 101, a sign to be in the field of my heart. Or I am feeling a charge against a situation and suddenly I hear on the radio the station identification for FM 103, a signal to call in a field of neutrality through Field 103 and compassionate empathy.

KORVIT/SHUTTERSTOCK

Other ways divine alignments can express may be through symbols randomly "appearing" in our love holograms. Any symbol that presents itself repeatedly in our awareness can serve as a form of divine alignment. Our chosen symbol to signal Field of 111 is the North Star, or it can be any symbol you feel a current connection to at this moment.

For me, Field 111 is currently signaled through a penny. Yes, a penny, a simple, small coin that is part of my everyday currency in life is my sign of divine alignment and flow.

IGOR ZH./SHUTTERSTOCK

NATALI GLADO/SHUTTERSTOCK

Why a penny? Recently I experienced a form of Field 111 through a penny. Over a series of several days, I kept finding "random" pennies. One penny was sitting on my kitchen stove with no explanation for how it found its way there. Then I was running and found a penny in the pocket of my running shorts. Next I noticed a penny was affixed right under the tire of my car, then on the sidewalk, and then in the dirt by a sprinkler. At this point, I began to pay attention.

What message was being reflected back to me in my love hologram through the repetitive random appearance of pennies? As the meaning-maker in my hologram, it could be a literal placeholder to signal that I may need to keep track of all my pennies, as money may be scarce and spare change would add up. I did not resonate with that notion, as it was based in fear, not love.

I then considered that the penny could be a sign of the field of abundance (often noted through Field 106). Find a penny, pick it up, all day long, we have good luck. Good luck is a form of abundance.

Yet I sensed I was not really getting the deeper meaning of the penny symbolism in my love hologram. If I knew how this penny was showing up to make me more aware of divine alignment (Field 111) in my love hologram, what might I realize?

Was I perhaps discounting all the recent small changes in my life? Was I not recognizing how massive each little change could be in terms of rippling overall change into my entire love hologram? I felt excited at this possible interpretation. This was a sign to me to pay closer attention to the pennies as signs of divine alignment, small signs of useful change that add up to significant shifts in my love hologram.

Suddenly I recalled that I used to collect pennies in a jar when I was a teenager. This random associative memory also held a key piece for me in regard to processing a big situational change I am experiencing now. Thus recognizing divine alignments can be as simple as loose change.

Drop down into the field of your heart, if you choose, and center in your love hologram. Signal intent to connect to Field 111, Divine Alignment and Synchronicity. If you were to be more aware of synchronicity as a sign of flow and connection, what might occur to you? How might you notice more divine alignments as a result of connecting to Field 111? Write this down, if you choose. Then pay attention when anything related to what you have noted appears in your life.

Now, choose a symbol that represents your personal connection to Field 111. Take note of this symbol and write it down for easy remembering. The symbol may be a repetitive number, such as 111 or 33 or 888, or it may be a feather, or a special coin, or a certain song.

Now, over the next few weeks, pay attention to the appearance of this symbol in your love holo-gram. How often do you notice it? What are you thinking, doing, experiencing, when this symbol for Field 111 shows up?

To be more aware of the presence of synchron-icity and divine alignments in your life, consider carrying this symbol with you as you go about your daily routine. If you cannot carry the actual symbol, then the word or a picture will suffice as a placeholder for the symbol.

Allow for the chosen symbol to represent your conscious connection to Field 111, so you can experience more flow, more fulfillment, and more connection. Divine alignment can be a sign as small as a penny or as big as the North Star reflecting back to us that all is well. Indeed, we are on the right path, and we are facing our true north, as we live from our hearts with integrity, flowing as one peace with change, present in our lives one moment at a time.

$\mathcal{F}$112

Speak Your Truth. True Authentic Expression.

Field 112 supports us in easily speaking our truth and expressing our unique perspective of reality, as we choose to do. This Field establishes resonance with our natural ability to express the truths of our heart–mind intelligence.

This Field also supports us in living our truth as a True Authentic Expression of our TAS and allowing this to be reflected in all endeavors. This means showing our true colors and living as vibrantly as we may choose. True Authentic Expression is as much about speaking authentically as it is about embodying a state of integrity in relation to our TAS. This Field supports us in being able to express ourselves in relation to other individuals, groups, structures, and Fields.

Our chosen symbol for this Field is a peacock. Peacocks are proud to strut their stuff and display

RICKYD/SHUTTERSTOCK

their unique feathers. They do not apologize for being "pea-cocky," as this is not arrogance but rather a confidence that comes from being exactly who they are in every moment. Peacocks speak volumes about authenticity as integrity without ever uttering a word.

As this Field is about more than speaking truth and includes embodying truth, a peacock can help us symbolically connect to Field 112 when we need assistance either hearing ourselves or seeing ourselves so that others can hear and see us too.

The practice of True Authentic Expression is a natural progression that occurs as a result of loving and living as True Authentic Self. Field 112, represented by a peacock, can help us create new ways of expressing ourselves based on the truth within our hearts. This Field supports expressing preferences and living out those preferences in our love holograms—in other words, creating your own style of being, and then decorating your love hologram accordingly without apology or compromise. All expressions can be symmetric expressions of authenticity by virtue of connecting to Field 112.

All expressions can be perfectly imperfect just like the patterning of even the most elegant peacock feathers.

Field 112 supports speaking truth and living truth. Drop into the field of the heart and center in your Love Sphere, if you choose. Connect to Field 101 if you need support.

Consider a situation in your life where you do not authentically express yourself either verbally or in your actions. Connect to that pattern now. Notice what thoughts, feelings, sensations, or experiences come into your awareness. How do you feel now as you relate to these patterns? Write down whatever occurs to you, if you choose.

Now signal Field 112 and allow for the symbol of a peacock to come into your awareness. Notice the beauty of this reflection. Ask yourself what it would feel like now to confidently live as your True Authentic Expression and speak your truth in the same way a peacock proudly displays its feathers in daily endeavors. Feel that connection now. Write down any thoughts, sensations, perceptions, or experiences that occur for you.

If you knew what was holding you back from fully opening into Field 112, and your own True Authentic Expression, what would occur to you? Write this down, if you choose.

It may be appropriate to signal other Fields at this time, for additional assistance. Fields 103, 107, 108, and 109, or any Field that occurs to you, may help. Simply connect to any Field that feels useful in addition to Field 112. Additional Fields are not needed, but they are always welcome, like additional friends joining a playful party.

From the field of the heart, share with yourself how resonance with Field 112 can favorably change up how you have configured your love hologram. Write down anything that occurs to you. Take note when this happens. Feel free to connect to Field 112 and the symbol of a peacock any time you need a little encouragement to clearly articulate thoughts, ideas, or emotions. Feel free to connect to Field 112 when you want to honor True Authentic Expression without fear. Field 112 is always near for articulations and actions that are vibrant and clear.

$\mathcal{F}$113

True Authentic Relating (TAR).

True Authentic Relating (TAR) can be a sticky situation, or it can be the substance of love that bonds us with others on our varied life paths. TAR is a natural side effect of living as, and loving, our True Authentic Self (TAS).

In fact, True Authentic Relating is simply creating reflections of true authenticity in our interpersonal relations with others. Although there are no rules for TAR, a facet of this experience, and thus of resonance with this Field, is a willingness to be vulnerable—a willingness to be seen and heard coupled with a willingness to see and hear others.

Field 113 supports our ability to Truly Authentically Relate to self, others, and all that we are "in relation to" in our love holograms. This Field recognizes that TAR first begins with selves and then ripples outward. Thus this field supports honesty, integrity, presence, and forgiveness, all facets of vulnerability. True Authentic Relating opens us to Love and Grace and a willingness to show up for the conversation, no matter what.

Often we avoid TAR for fear of rejection, fear of confrontation, and fear of whatever imagined negative potential outcome might transpire. Nonetheless, often we fail to recognize that each time we do not show up for TAR, we betray ourselves. Field 113 supports us in feeling empowered to lovingly engage with others from our hearts based on what feels right, true, and correct for us in the moment, while remaining open to receiving what feels right, true, and correct for others.

This Field also supports choice with discernment, as not all scenarios are appropriate platforms for TAR.

Everyone has a desire to be seen and heard as he or she truly is. Yet not everyone is willing to be seen and heard. Not every organization or group is open to TAR, so sometimes this Field can teach us when it is time to move away from a structure we may be supporting when that structure does not support us.

Field 113 supports our ability to intuit relating with discernment and provides us with the strength and courage to find our tribe where TAR is possible, available, appreciated, and welcome.

This Field also supports us in realizing that TAR does not necessarily require two parties for this to occur. In other words, TAR is our responsibility, and how another reacts to TAR is not up to us. It is up to us to center in our hearts with openness. Openness is the invitation for another to step into TAR as a safe experience that does not bind anyone to sticky outcomes but rather liberates all in love's reflection. This liberation is based on equality, respect, and dignity.

Practicing TAR can be a bit like penguins trying to pass eggs on ice. TAR is an art of delicate balance, a dance of grace that is perfectly synchronized when we are present. Presence is key to TAR, or else the momentary opportunity may be lost to all dropped eggs of past relations.

For this reason, our chosen symbol for Field 113 is a waddling penguin with happy feet. (You may choose a different symbol of preference.) Penguins are a beautiful testimony to teamwork, shared purpose, and a willingness to work through challenges, all components of True Authentic Relating and Field 113.

Penguins stand strong in their True Authentic Power, and they have a resilience that enables them to thrive in even the most challenging of circumstances. TAR can be challenging at times, as love and rigid notions of reality are both bound between the parameters of individuals. Field 113 and penguin wiggles can remind us to be flexible as we relate to others, and Field 113 can assist us in doing the same.

KOTOMITI OKUMA/SHUTTERSTOCK

Penguins are highly intuitive creatures who seem to know when to waddle away and swim in a different pool of direction. Sometimes TAR can teach us that it is time to find new waters and new territories for living, loving, creating, and experiencing in our love holograms.

Penguins are also very adept at perceiving things in new ways. Technically, penguins are not able to fly, but that does not seem to stop them. Penguins exhibit tremendous trust in their selves and their surroundings. Similarly, Field 113 can teach us to trust in ourselves as we relate to others, groups, and organizations. We can experience TAR based on new possibilities, not frozen ideas of past experiences.

Practical Play with TAR is something that is unique to everyone. To experience TAR is to experience the beauty of love dancing with self and others. Sometimes it may feel like a struggle, but it is always worthwhile to honor ourselves as we relate to ourselves and others.

Drop down into the field of the heart, and center in your Love Sphere, if you choose. Consider a situ-

82

ation or circumstance in your life now where more TAR would be welcome to you. Write down what occurs to you, if you choose. Now, simply project the image of the chosen situation or circumstance into a new Love Sphere directly in front of you.

How might connection to Field 113 support you in relating to this experience in different, more empowering and liberating ways? Write down any ideas that occur to you, or notice how the projected image in front of you is already changing now.

Signal Field 113, TAR, and leverage the symbol of penguins together. Allow them to enter into the Love Sphere in front of you.

If the penguins were to interact with the chosen circumstance to model TAR for you, what attributes and characteristics would they display? Would they be more playful, spontaneous, and trusting? Would they demonstrate trust of the heart by focusing on the delicate egg of emotions often shared and conveyed in TAR with loving care and presence?

Would they be fearless and willing to be vulnerable as they encounter new terrains to play, rather than remembering past slips on the ice? How can these aspects of the Penguins' Way support you in resonating more strongly with Field 113 so you can experience more TAR in your love hologram?

If you were to leverage Field 113 at home, in social settings, and perhaps even at work, what would be different for you? How might this Field of TAR support you in experiencing more flow, joy, and fulfillment in your endeavors? Play with the Field of TAR like a new friend, and be amazed at how easily the stifling ice melts and pools of love surround us. Simply start TAR now.

F114

True Authentic Beauty (TAB) at Home in All Bodies.

This Field supports us in sacred vessel appreciation of our physical body as well as cohesive alignment with all our bodies, including mental, emotional, spiritual, and etheric/causal bodies.

Field 114 allows us to restore harmony and regenerate vitality and clarity in all layers of our being, so we may be at home in all matters.

We can leverage this Field to come into greater coherency with all our bodies. For example, I may feel good physically, but emotionally I may be disassociated from myself or my created scenarios. Perhaps emotionally I am content, but mentally I am distracted. This Field supports PRESENCE as a gift at all levels of being.

Field 114 supports our ability to appreciate our bodies in general. It is far too easy to critique our flaws. This Field helps us to appreciate our True Authentic Beauty. Keep TABs on how you talk to your body. Field 114 supports loving body and loving self-talk.

Others have shared the following in relation to Field 114:

> When I feel like any of my body needs support (emotionally, physically, mentally, spiritually) I call on Field 114 to return to homeostasis. I also love to snuggle my kids at night and call Field 114 to help their sweet bodies.
>
> Calling in 114 for a couple of days in a row while observing the patterns around having gained weight has reshaped attitudes and habits. The weight is effortlessly leaving, and I'm enjoying walking and smaller portions. All of it feels like play!

The chosen symbol for this Field is the starfish. A starfish is a symbol of eternal love and yet also represents regeneration. As many know, a remarkable property of a starfish is its ability to regenerate limbs and, essentially, any part of its body. We too are like starfish, capable of regenerating our bodies, whether they be physical, mental, emotional, spiritual, or etheric/causal bodies. At home in all bodies is supported by resonance with this Field.

Drop down into the field of heart and center in your Love Sphere, if you choose. Allow for the symbol of a starfish to appear in your awareness. If you prefer, you may center the starfish in a Love Sphere in front of you. Now connect to this star

NETFALLS - REMY MUSSER/SHUTTERSTOCK

fish as a signal of intent to activate Field 114, Field Flow.

Allow for each of the five arms on the starfish to represent all bodies: physical, mental, emotional, spiritual, and etheric/causal bodies. Pay attention as you label each arm and notice what each arm does with the information. Does the physical arm get shorter? Is the emotional arm entirely missing? Are the mental and spiritual arms twisted together like pretzels? Anything that occurs is perfect. Write down anything that comes to your awareness, if you choose.

Follow your imagination and allow curiosity to guide you through this Practical Play. How does the information provided through the starfish correspond to circumstances unfolding in your love hologram? Have you been working too hard and not getting enough rest and creative play time and so your physical starfish arm is short on vitality? Have you perhaps been ignoring your emotions (and intuitions) about a pattern in your life and so your starfish arm is totally missing in action, absent from connection with all other arms of your total body? Are you possibly compartmentalizing your spiritual essence into a mental framework that is creating a pretzeling of these two pivotal bodies of information?

While maintaining connection to Field 114, invite the field to regenerate any of the arms of your starfish. Allow for clear, cohesive signaling to bring forth symmetry in your starfish. What thoughts, sensations, perceptions, or experiences occur for you during this reconfiguring process? Write down anything that occurs to you, if you choose.

Call on Field 114 any time you need more love in any one or all of your interconnected bodies. You are a star, and the starfish reminds us to swim in the sea of our hearts with the power to regenerate and transform how we relate to all our bodies of information. Sacred vessel appreciation the starfish way.

$\mathcal{F}$115

Mother Matters.

Field 115 supports a coherent and congruent relationship with Mother Creator through Mother Relater. Trust. Trust of self in relation to self. Trust of self in relation to mother. Trust of self in relation to other. Trust in the universe. This Field relates to our mothers, being a mother, not being a mother, never being mothered, being over-mothered, and mothers-in-law too. This Field includes cohesive relationships with all aspects of Mother Nature and nurturing matters.

This is a field of trust and supports self-love and self-nurturing, a form of mothering in relation to self. Field 115 clears rifts in relation to all mothering matters for men and women alike.

Field 115 also supports transforming misappropriated energies and distorted grids in the collective consciousness pertaining to the divine feminine, projected and reflected in all mothering relations and all surrogate fields of control.

Field 115 supports all forms of mothering, whether that is of a child, a business, a project, or a personal need. Mother energy is within us all as potential power. When we clear up resonance with distorted templates of mother matters, the creative potential of that mother energy is catalyzed in our love holograms and is reflected in all matters.

The chosen symbol for this Field of Mother Matters is the lily flower. Lilies can represent portals to Field 115 to help clear issues related to femininity while activating creativity, receptivity, intuition, compassion, and love. Lilies, a beacon for Field 115, offer women and men an opening into a more compassionate way of being. This way of being is inclusive, communal, and nurturing.

This Field and the lily symbol also support a clearing of outmoded ways of relating to concepts of the sacred feminine. There is a movement beyond wounded feminine and reactive feminine into whole feminine, which includes the masculine as part of itself. This Field supports us in embracing the sacred feminine within everything.

Playing in Field 115 can have an immediate effect on how we feel about ourselves, our mothers, other women, and fields that have traditionally disempowered women and men both as a form of surrogate (false) control.

We may feel a sense of trust, nurtured by the womb of creation in an eternally loving universe,

LOTUS IMAGES/SHUTTERSTOCK

when we connect to Field 115. This is a field of cele-
bration for all mother matters. We celebrate our
ability to mother self, and we celebrate all modes
of mothering that motivate us to create and actu-
alize in our love holograms.

Drop down into the field of the heart and center
in your Love Sphere. Signal Field 101 for support,
if you choose.

Consider an issue regarding mother matters
that you want to change in your life and feel into
the pattern now. What thoughts, feelings, sensations, perceptions, or experiences come into your
awareness? Write these down, if you choose. Now,
signal intent to connect to Field 115, Mother
Matters, and see a lily in your love hologram as a
symbol of your connection to this Field of trust.

If the lily were to speak to you about this
chosen pattern and how connecting to Field 115
can change how you relate to mother matters, what
might the lily say? Does the lily speak of self-trust,
forgiveness, and appreciation of self and All mothering matters? Does the lily invite you to blossom
into your own femininity and to integrate this

91

flow-ering with the masculine energies naturally within us all?

Does the lily speak to your heart, whispering self-empowerment, not as a form of control over anything but as a function of inner dominion and flow with the formless eternal love of divine feminine energy that sustains all? Whatever messages, thoughts, ideas, or sensations that occur to you, allow them to percolate in your awareness, and write them down, if you choose. Invite each notion to spin in your love hologram until you choose to embody them as a whole part of self.

Pay close attention to how the chosen pattern changes as a result of resonance with Field 115. Notice the Flow. Notice the Trust. Notice the lily as many times as you choose to support a continued conscious connection to the Field of Mother Matters.

$\mathcal{F}_{116}$

True Authentic Desire (TAD) Pleasure (Play-Sure).

True Authentic Desires (TAD) are genuine desires that well up from the field of the heart. True Authentic Desires are cues from universal consciousness to pay attention, for when allowed to unfold, TADs manifest as magnificence.

Field 116 supports us in activating our True Authentic Desires. A True Authentic Desire (TAD) is what inspires you. What inspires you is what brings you joy. Joy is sunshine for the TAD seed and its nurturing soil, signaling rays of play-sure for the power of love as life. The Joy of Being is reflected from the sunshine of your heart into the heart of the seed idea of TADs. Two hearts signal as One as your heart and seed idea dance together in spiraling waves of grace, as together they express finite forms of distinctions from infinite formlessness. True Authentic Desires are holographic seeds of completion, born into existence by deeds of action and experience.

This Field is also a field of PLAY-sure, as in sensuality and juiciness. Field 116 supports us in connecting to our own nectar, our own flowing love that nourishes all endeavors.

Our chosen symbol for this Field is a seed. This seed is planted in the nurturing soil of a garden, watered regularly with attention, activated and delighted by the sunshine of joy in our love holograms.

Connection to Field 116 can also support us in determining our TADs. What brings us joy? Many may not know the answer stemming from inner truth, for the sunshine of joy may be clouded by programs of confusion, distortion, and others' expectations.

Field 116 can help us recognize TAD seeds from the weeds of programming so we can pick the weeds out of our garden to create space in our soil for the TAD seeds to blossom.

Drop down into the field of heart and center in your Love Sphere. Signal Field 101 if you need assistance. Consider something that may be a TAD and allow for a symbol, color, or object to come into your awareness that represents this TAD. Connect to the symbol now, and feel into it as though it already IS fully blossomed in your love hologram.

Now signal intent to connect to Field 116, TAD PLAY-sure. Allow for the chosen Field symbol of

CHEPKO DANIL VITALEVICH/SHUTTERSTOCK

the seed to pop into your awareness, representing Field 116. While remaining connected to the image of the chosen TAD and the seed, see an area of garden soil in front of you, and choose a place to plant the seed. As you plant the seed, soon to be watered with loving intent and nurtured by the light of the sun, plant the symbol of TAD completion with the seed symbol of Field 116. Nestle the symbols together as though they are hugging as one.

Together the seed of potential and the projection of TAD as completion will grow, reflecting symmetric waves of love to fully blossom into actualization and experience. As you remain connected to Field 116, this TAD seed and potential manifestation, what actions can you take and what choices can you make to nurture this seed, to water its soil and support rays of joy signaling growth toward full bloom? Write down any ideas, thoughts, sensations, experiences, or plans that may occur to you.

Feel free also to leverage this Field as nectar for notions, to give juice to ideas as impetus for actions. Visit your garden daily and water the seeds.

Lovingly shine light upon the soil and open your heart to the connection between seed of potential and seed of completion, growing together as One. Remember to take action to support cultivation of this TAD. Bring in any of the other Fields for support as doing so may occur to you.

All TADs are seeds of completion. Pay Attention and PLAY attention (without tension) to TADs, fueled by the juice of PLAY-sure through Field 116, and allow for TADs to blossom into reflections of magnificence in your love hologram.

𝓕117

Playing Agelessly.

Field 117 recognizes that a new age happens in every new moment, and the beauty of time is that it is an Eternal Spiral of love. This Field is about forming a new relationship to time where linear living expands to limitless loving no matter our chronological age. Field 117 supports the embrace of time as comprising distinctions in consciousness based on living in the eternal now.

Resonance with Field 117 creates new ways to relate to the aging process, in terms of progressions of wisdom and distinctions of experience. Through the eyes of innocent perception, each moment is new, and each movement is created through the eternal you. Living and loving agelessly is to employ the art of PLAY flowing into each moment no matter what our chronological age.

CRANACH/SHUTTERSTOCK

Our chosen symbol to represent this Field is the swan. The swan is a symbol for grace and eternal love. It can also represent balance and commitment. Field 117 supports love of self at all points of reference in time and a commitment to the inner beauty and intuitive wisdom of the timeless heart, rather than focusing on external standards set by certain societal expectations.

Aging is a morphic field, and like a swan, we can gracefully swim toward resonance with eternal fields of love that do not follow the limitations of linear time.

Swans remind us of the beauty of being and flowing in the moment. Their graceful swimming style leaves hardly a ripple in the pond. This does not mean that you should not make waves; rather, this means you should leave no ripple behind. As time passes, nothing is ever lost or forgotten. Our movements, choices, and experiences always flow with us when we swim gently with the currents of our lives without resistance.

Drop down into the field of the heart and center in your Love Sphere. Connect to Field 101 for support, if you choose. Now, consider a situation in your life that seems to have something to do with aging or the so-called distant past. It may be something you are experiencing, or it may be in relation to a family member or even a global field related to growing older. Choose a symbol to represent this pattern. It may be an image of the pattern or a word or color that comes to mind. Project this symbol out in front of your love hologram either inside or outside the parameters of your Love Sphere. Choose what feels comfortable for you.

As you connect to this pattern, notice any thoughts, feelings, sensations, or experiences that come to your awareness. Write these down, if you choose.

Intend to connect to Field 117, Playing Agelessly, and allow for the symbol of a swan to emerge in your awareness adjacent to the symbol of the chosen pattern. As you connect to the swan, as a symbol for signaling Field 117, invite yourself to open to the beauty and grace of this magical, graceful creature. Remaining connected, allow for the image of the swan to merge with the chosen pattern of concern, solutions of which are all available in the eternal now.

As the two symbols merge together as one, what do you notice? What thoughts, feelings, sensations, or experiences come to your awareness? Write these down, if you choose. How does connection to Field 117 through the symbol of the swan support the pattern you have chosen to focus on, interact with, and modify resonance? How might continued connection to Field 117 allow for additional changes to ripple out into your love hologram? You may stay connected to Field 117, as with all Fields, as long as you choose. The symbol of the swan will be there always to represent your opening into a field of playing timelessly.

$\mathcal{F}118$

PLAY—*Potential Love Awaiting You.*

PLAY is Potential Love Awaiting You.

This is a field of creative flexibility and camaraderie with self and others. Field 118 facilitates an ease of access to play without an agenda or the need to accomplish anything. In this Field, we are able to readily become like little children with childlike wonder and innocent perception. In this state of being, we are dazzled by what may happen in the very next moment. This Field supports our ability to PLAY, which brings forth our joy and reestablishes flow.

PLAY takes us out of our thoughts and puts us in our hearts. A space of play is a place (play-ce) where anything may happen. From this space of heart-centered awareness, we have access to all.

Our chosen symbol for Field 118 is little children playing joyfully together anywhere. Perhaps

CONRADO/SHUTTERSTOCK

they are at the beach or in a park, or simply in a room together. Children can bring alive their surroundings with imaginative delight. When children PLAY, they are in the moment, without regard for what happened yesterday or what may happen tomorrow. Play is awareness of creative intelligence expressing Now. Our ability to PLAY opens when we embrace the magical, childlike wonder that is eternally within us all.

This Field is also a field of friendship with self and others. Our ability to be our own best friend and then a True Authentic Friend to others is supported through resonance with Field 118.

Collaboration cannot exist freely when forces of control are at play. Collaboration flourishes through graceful commands from the field of the heart—gentle-handed movements of unity expressing through diversity. This is also a Field that supports collaboration. Collaboration is community sharing through individuality. Share in the calm-unity of community. Collaborate, celebrate, and co-create.

RAWPIXEL.COM/SHUTTERSTOCK

Drop down into the field of the heart and center in your Love Sphere. Signal Field 101 if additional support may seem useful. Now, consider some areas or circumstances in your life that are seemingly devoid of PLAY. Perhaps it is a work scenario or a way of relating to someone in your family. Perhaps it is simply your weekly chores, such as cleaning the house and doing dishes. Or consider a pattern where friendship to self and others could be amplified.

Signal your intent to connect to Field 118, PLAY. Bring forth into your love hologram the image of the chosen symbol for Field 118: children playing together. Perhaps the children are building sand castles at the beach or playing hide and seek at the park. Or perhaps they are simply playing a game of magical make-believe and together their awareness is aboard a ship at sea or in a castle atop a mountain in a kingdom far, far away. Whatever comes to mind as you evoke the image of children playing, trust it.

As you connect to Field 118, ask yourself how the Field of PLAY can favorably influence the circumstances that seem to be devoid of PLAY. How can modeling childlike wonder, innocent perception, friendship with self and others, and friendship with the universe change up your configured experiences in your love hologram? Write down any thoughts, sensations, emotions, or experiences that occur for you as you connect to the Field 118, PLAY: Potential Love Awaiting You. Do not wait. Access this loving Field now, anytime, and always.

F119

Be Your Own Light.

Field 119 supports resonant awareness, flow, and ease of grace in being your own light. Choose to radiate the light and joy that you are as an authentically empowered way of being, despite contrast and projections, shadows, distortions, and limited reflections.

Continue to shine your light regardless of what external placeholders in awareness may be projecting into the love hologram. Field 119 enables us all to no longer dim our light or keep it hidden so someone (or something) may feel brighter.

Light Radiates. Field 119 supports the brilliance of the light that is limitless love in shining, regardless of what seems to be happening (or not happening) in any given moment. Shine on and be the sine wave for love.

ARIDOCEAN/SHUTTERSTOCK

Our chosen symbol for Field 119 is the seahorse. The seahorse tail is in the ratio of the golden mean spiral and has a strength to stay connected to any location weathering rough currents and stormy seas. The seahorse, though not fast, is very stealthy. It has a stability to it, suggesting contentment in being what it is.

And those seahorses that dare to be their own light can light up even the darkest layers of the deepest seas. A special type of seahorse (*Hippocampus erectus*) has an ability to be its own light in a form of radiation known as biofluorescence. The seahorse is able to radiate light in the deepest, darkest waters of reality. Like the brilliant seahorse, we may do the same.

Be Your Own Light is a Field that reminds us not to dim our light so others can be brighter. Resonance with Field 119 can support us in embodying the Light that we are and Shining Bright no matter what. We do not need to dim our brilliance for another person (or structure) to seem brighter. We do not need to shade our radiating essence so as to fit in with the shadows of contrast and the darker crevices of our reality.

Drop down into the field of the heart and center in your Love Sphere. Signal Field 101 for assistance as needed.

From the field of the heart, consider a situation or circumstance where you are currently dimming your own light. Perhaps you are afraid to be seen, or you may be playing small so others may feel unnaturally bigger. However you may be dimming your light, connect to the pattern. What thoughts, feelings, sensations, or experiences surface for you as you consider this pattern? Notice whatever honestly comes up for you, and write this down, if you choose.

If you know why you may have developed this strategy to dim your light, what occurs to you? Write this down, if you choose. Feel free to include any feelings or thoughts of rejection, alienation, or fear. Whatever it is that you discover and reveal to yourself, allow for that to be OK. It is all OK.

Now, signal intent to connect to Field 119. Leverage the symbol of a glowing seahorse in the night ocean as a conscious way to connect to Field 119. With the symbol of the seahorse floating in your love hologram, ask how Field 119 can support you in being your own light, no matter what is happening. Write down any thoughts, feelings, sensations, or experiences that occur to you, if you choose.

How may Field 119 and the symbol of the radiating seahorse support you in relating to others moving forward, where, previously, you may have dimmed your light?

If you could know what it would feel like to shine bright in your love hologram, what experiences would be different for you? Connect now to what it feels like for you to shine as bright as the seahorse in all that you relate to in your love hologram. Bravo for your bravery in being your own light.

Signal the seahorse and Field 119 any time you may need support and strength to remind you that being your own light is an integral part of being who you truly are; to embrace this unique light (no matter what) is to experience the joy of being . . . you! Dare to be seen. Dare to shine. Field 119: Be your own light, and the biofluorescent seahorse will always leave the light on for you, too!

$\mathcal{F}$120

***I Love You AND . . . No. I Love You AND . . . Yes.
Unconditional Love Does Not Mean Loving All
Conditions.***

Field 120 supports resonance with unconditional love experienced through conditions and the ability to say no from a loving, graceful space in the heart.

Unconditional love does not mean loving all conditions. Unconditional love does not mean that we need to tolerate all circumstances to prove that we can love unconditionally. Unconditional love does not need us to prove anything. Unconditional love has no conditions.

However, unconditional love in relation to conditions has parameters. Conditions are not placed on the love itself. Conditions are only placed on the circumstances that we are willing, or not willing, to show up for in relation to self and others.

DANIEL-LIFE/SHUTTERSTOCK

Our chosen symbol for this field is the dragonfly. The dragonfly can symbolize change in perspective and a form of self-realization; this kind of change is a form of mental and emotional maturity that reflects self-love.

The dragonfly, with amazing ability to skim the surface of water while during flight, invites us to look beneath the surface of our patterned ways of relating to discover a deeper meaning about self-love in relation to ourselves.

This creature has an amazing property of iridescence on both of its wings as well as on its body. Iridescence is the ability of an object to show itself in different colors, depending on the angle and polarization of light falling on it. We may be like the dragonfly in our ability to assume different identities in relation to loving others. However, our true colors are always reflected when we love and live from the field of the heart.

Field 120 and the symbol of the dragonfly remind us to be transparent as TAS and not to take on the colors of the patterns we may be associating with in the name of so-called unconditional love.

We get to choose what colors reflect off our wings, and we choose our True Authentic Colors. We choose TAS.

The dragonfly is a symbol of speed, dexterity, and grace. It has an ability to move in all six directions and can move at a speed of up to forty-five miles an hour. Furthermore, the dragonfly can hover like a helicopter before flying backward—all while minimally flapping its wings. The dragonfly is efficient in its ability to move in a chosen direction.

Without wavering in the wind, the dragonfly exhibits clarity, efficiency, and a grace of movement away from undesired circumstances toward where it has determined it wants to go.

Resonance with Field 120 and connecting to this Field through the chosen symbol of the dragonfly can support us in recognizing that loving unconditionally does not mean we must hover in intolerable circumstances.

Our TAS, like the iridescent dragonfly, is able to say I love you and . . . no this doesn't work for me. I love you and . . . though I can fly backward with you, or in a plethora of chaotic directions (in any direction, actually), I am not congruent with your chosen flight path, and so I choose to fly a different way.

Field 120 supports us in being able to skim the surface of a flight pattern too and to see beneath it to its real underlying meaning in relation to loving self. Perhaps we think that loving unconditionally means we have to prove ourselves by showing we can tolerate anything. Field 120 will reveal a new light through our wings so we can take flight in different, more empowering and liberating ways. This does not mean that we stop relating to those we are in flight with; rather, this means we relate in new ways, from different angles, with a precision and grace that is the expression of our "True Authentic Self."

Drop down into the field of the heart and center in your Love Sphere. Signal Field 101 for additional support, if you choose.

Consider a pattern in your life where you may be struggling with reconciling that loving unconditionally may include not loving all conditions. Perhaps you are unable to recognize this important distinction, and so you feel guilty or judgmental of self and others.

How might Field 120 support you in freely realizing that love does not mean loving all situations. "I love you and . . . no this does not work for me." "I love you and . . . yes this works for me." If you were able to notice and experience this Now, how would your experience already be different? How does I love you AND open you into neverANDing possibilities?

Signal intent to connect to Field 120 and leverage the symbol of a dragonfly to represent this particular Field. If you prefer another symbol, feel free to choose another symbol. As you consider the pattern you may be struggling with, choose a symbol of word to represent this pattern, and project this in front of you directly outside of your Love Sphere.

Allow for the dragonfly as a symbol for Field 120 (or whatever symbol you may have chosen) to begin interacting with the pattern. Which parts of the pattern is the dragonfly OK with, as a reflection of what you are OK with too? Allow for the dragonfly to carry those OK parts that you lovingly accept into your Love Sphere.

When the dragonfly has completed this process, watch the dragonfly return to the chosen pattern and hover over the remaining parts of the pattern just outside your Love Sphere.

Notice which parts of the pattern the dragonfly is not OK with, as a reflection of what you are not OK with too. These parts that are remaining are the parts of the pattern called "I love you and . . . NO thank you." You do not need to allow these components, situations, circumstances, into your love hologram to prove you are able to Love Unconditionally.

How does connection with Field 120 and the symbol of the dragonfly support you in being able to discern the difference between love and circumstances? Write down any thoughts, emotions, sensations, or experiences that occur for you as a result of this question. Anything that occurs to you is OK and acceptable. What is honest is OK.

How does Field 120 enable you to honor TAS and all you may relate to in a way that says I am love and that does not mean I am aligned, congruent, or in full integrity with these choices. I choose to fly over here on a chosen path that is a more symmetric reflection of my TAS. I love you and I say no to you so I may say yes to myself. Signal Field 120 and the symbol of the dragonfly whenever you need clear light for your flight. Signal this field for support in saying I Love you and . . . no. I Love you and . . . yes!

$\mathcal{F}$121

Done as Distinctions.

What Is Done?

What is done? There are many, many, many layers to being done. Each time we may think we are completely done with a pattern, a new level of done may surface. This new level provides another set of distinctions to be made from another angle of the holographic prism that was not previously noticed. It is akin to looking at a diamond from a new side, from a new angle in different light, where different intricacies as informational patterns are reflected as awareness.

At the fully transformative level, done means that the patterns that we were entangled with that were preventing us from fully completely loving unconditionally have been released.

At this level of transformation, done is so complete that there is no longer any perceived pain around the experience. It is as though we have looked at a pattern from every angle and made myriad distinctions such that awareness of the geometric grid of the pattern is complete. Field 121, Done, supports us in being done with patterns in our personal perspective realities that do not reflect the diamond brilliance of self-love in relation to . . . anything.

Various layers of done as distinctions are profiled extensively in *Little Book of Big Potentials*. For a greater understanding of where you may be in the Field of Done, please refer to that book now for more information.

Our chosen symbol for Field 121 is a diamond. All diamonds are perfect in their own brilliance. Different cuts reflect different angles of light, depending on our perspectives. Every pattern in our love holograms has a diamond-like quality, offering us the ability to make new distinctions in our awareness. We may discover clarity, and wisdom about ourselves, and that which we are in relation to, through the diamond-like prism of Field 121.

Drop down into the field of the heart and center in your Love Sphere. Signal Field 101 for assistance, as needed. Signal intent to connect to Field 121, Done, and project the image of a diamond in front of you, just outside of your Love Sphere.

POSTERIORI/SHUTTERSTOCK

Now, consider a pattern you want to be done with. Assign a symbol to this pattern. It may be an image, or a word, or even a color. Project that symbol into the diamond image in front of you.

Reference the various levels of Done as Distinctions shared freely in *Little Book of Big Potentials*. What category of Done as Distinctions do you most closely relate to as you consider this pattern in front of you?

Now, as you look upon this pattern in the diamond connecting you to Field 121, turn the diamond any which way you choose so that different angles of the pattern may be reflected and different angles of awareness may come to light.

What aspects of the pattern do you notice now from a new angle that you did not previously recognize? Write these down, if you choose. What part of the Done Configuration does this new prism of awareness represent? Turn the pattern again for a different angle of awareness and insight. Turn the diamond again for another new insight, if you choose. Write down any and all insights reflected in your Done Diamond.

117

How many parts of this diamond pattern seem to reveal not being done as an invitation for self-love? How does loving self as Self-IS and connection to Field 121 allow for the various facets of the not done pattern to reveal themselves now, to transform now, to release and reconfigure now?

Done is already begun. What would the diamond look like if you were already done as in Done Done? Reflect on this brilliance. Connect to Field 121 and Done as Diamond any time you need support in the illuminating diamond-like spectrum of Done.

$\mathcal{F}$122

Freedom from Addictions.

Field 122 supports the disconnection from habituated outloops of conditioned behavior that may express in the form of addictions as placeholders. Field 122 restores integrity, connection, and wholeness within the fragmented parts of awareness, eliciting, and perpetuating all addictive patterns.

All addictions are placeholders in awareness that represent an attempt to find True Authentic Self (TAS) and simultaneously avoid it. The placeholder that the addiction pattern represents serves as a habituated strategy to avoid recognizing self as an infinitely whole, perfect, and limitless being that is having an experience of limitation.

The pattern as placeholder serves as a habituated strategy to look for fulfillment and acceptance of TAS in something *outside of self* that is inherently and incessantly empty. In this recognition, there is freedom to recondition awareness and embrace integrity. There is freedom to move from dis-ease to flow in total acceptance, and to choose anew.

This is a field of freedom: freedom to be you and me, in the Joy of Being. Field 122 supports freedom from addictions as compulsions—freedom to live and love through the power of self-love and personal choice.

This field recognizes all addictions as opportunity—openings for integrous movement into the unity of an undivided self, cohesive, whole, and transparent.

Our chosen symbol for Field 122 is the butterfly. (You may choose a different symbol, if that is your preference.) The butterfly symbolizes freedom, transformation, and joy. The dance of the butterfly reflects an impetus for movement from where we are to our next phase of being.

Like a butterfly who evokes courage to break free from its cocoon, we need courage to let go of addictive behaviors, beyond our compulsions and habits of self-avoidance to open into a space of grace with choice. Field 122 and the symbol of the butterfly support us in the metamorphoses to freedom.

When the caterpillar first creates the cocoon, the caterpillar does not realize what is happening. When we first create our addictive patterns, we do not realize what is happening. We somehow become attached to our world of avoidance and

SUNS07BUTTERFLY/SHUTTERSTOCK

addictive ways of being but are not totally ready to enter a new world. We cocoon in our addictions. Our cocoon is essentially constructed from all the accumulated waste that is created in the wake of addictive patterns. The caterpillar must let go of this attachment to the cocoon to become a butterfly. We must let go of our attachment to hiding behind our addictive behaviors so that we may be free.

Like a caterpillar nested in a cocoon, the encapsulation of the addiction initially supports us and seemingly serves us. We are able to create a protective layer and barrier between our True Authentic Self (TAS) and the world, between our hearts and our truth, between our souls and our creations.

We are able to avoid seeing ourselves as love's reflection because all that we see is viewed through the lens of our addiction, our cocoon, our shelter for avoidance of transparency and authenticity.

Eventually our cocoon of habituated addiction feels stifling, for it prevents freedom of movement and new expressions beyond the confines of our molten addictions. Field 122 supports our movement from the false sense of safety created through addictive patterns into the love and freedom to fly as TAS.

This Field supports our metamorphose from caterpillar in cocoon to butterfly, without judgment and without excuses. There are no buts in becoming free from addiction. It simply is what we are entitled to experience as a movement for our souls' embodiment, our soul-utions.

Drop down into the field of the heart and center in your Love Sphere. Signal Field 101 for assistance, if you choose.

Consider a pattern in your life that you may be struggling with and that may be considered an addiction. For help on distinguishing between addictions and choices, please refer to the complete Field explanation shared in *Little Book of Big Potentials*.

Write down a brief description of this pattern, if you choose. What thoughts, sensations, emotions, or experiences often occur as a result of this repetitive behavior?

Do you feel isolated, confused, guilty, or full of regret following engagement with the behavior? Is the addiction the only way you can feel OK temporarily, followed by the experience of not feeling OK? Do you somehow feel helpless or paralyzed by an inability simply to stop? Do you feel stuck?

Do you feel a sense of pressure when you're not engaged in the addiction pattern—a pressure that seems it can only be relieved by the act of the addiction itself?

Whatever you feel, allow the emotion to surface and yourself to be in that feeling with honesty, and without shame.

Now signal intent to connect to Field 122, Freedom as Freedom from Addictions. Allow for the chosen symbol of the butterfly to appear inside your love hologram. This represents resonance with Field 122.

If you were to look to the butterfly for information about what awaits you on the other side of addiction, what might you notice? What aspects of freedom from addiction could the butterfly provide for you as an invitation to move from the cocoon of addiction to assume your wings and fly free?

When the butterfly was in its cocoon, it did not know what opportunities and vantage points were waiting beyond the transformation. Inside the cocoon, there was no view of what lay ahead in freedom. By tuning in to fields of information that provided the caterpillar with direction on how to move beyond the cocoon, therein emerged the butterfly.

Do not rely only on what you think you may know to get out of addictive patterns. Call on help, from the Fields, from the universe, and from other people. Many can lend guiding hands and helpful hugs, with loving light to illuminate the movements needed to fly free from the cocoon of addiction. Connection to Field 122 will signal a beacon for support from other butterflies to guide you. Know that you are not alone and that never do you need to resign yourself to always living stifled by the confines and cocoons of addictions.

Write down anything and everything that honestly occurs to you as you consider this addictive pattern and the Field of Freedom that is available to you if you choose. Just choose.

How might consistent connection to this Field starting NOW support you in movement away from compulsive behavior into the power of choice? How might leveraging Field 122 combined with other Fields support you even more? If you knew what Fields would be optimal for you to combine with Field 122, what would come to your awareness? Any and all of the Fields are available to help. Simply signal intent to connect and call forth the number of the Field or chosen symbol for that Field. Notice how connecting to more than one Field at a time can create an exponential effect.

Fly Free from addictive patterns with the support of Field 122. You are not your cocoon. You are not your addictions. You are love deserving to take flight on any path, like a butterfly. Fly free.

$\mathcal{F}$123

Soul Purpose. Life Purpose.

Field 123 supports resonance with our ability to live life's purpose, inspired by the soul, ignited by the field of the heart, activated by our creative will, and implemented through action.

Field 123 connects us to our divine blueprint and then brings forth that divine blueprint through the field of the heart, then through our minds (specifically our pineal glands) coupled to the ability to choose. This Field allows us to map our unique divine imprints into three-dimensional reality.

This Field offers us the courage to dare to dream, and then to dare to act to create the dream as an actualization into experience.

This Field facilitates embodying, living, and expressing our unique sole/soul signature as life purpose. Connection to this Field supports a reso-

SP-PHOTO/SHUTTERSTOCK

nant knowingness of our soul mission, our primary purpose for creating here in this embodiment.

Our chosen symbol for this Field is the pinecone. The spines of the pinecone spiral in a perfect Fibonacci sequence in either direction, much like a sunflower. The pine-al gland is shaped like (and named after) the pinecone. This gland is at the geometric center of the brain and is intimately linked to the body's perception of light. It is considered by many to be our biological third eye and the "seat of the soul."

Field 123 serves to activate our connection to our multidimensional awareness through both the field of the heart and the pineal gland together. Resonance with Field 123 allows for greater coherence with, and remembering of, our primary purpose for being here. Although our primary purpose may be love, we have additional specific missions to accomplish.

Drop down into the field of the heart and center in your Love Sphere. Consider what it would be like if you were really clear on what your life mission may be and how to live that mission more fully starting now.

Signal your intent to connect to Field 123. Do so by visualizing the chosen symbol of the pinecone directly above your head inside your Love Sphere. Connect your awareness from the field of the heart to the pinecone as a signal of resonance with Field 123. As you connect to the pinecone, see a white light emanating from the pinecone above your head down through the center of your head and then back down to the field of the heart. With this coherent light connection maintained, explore what thoughts, sensations, emotions, or experiences occur for you as you contemplate your soul mission. Write anything down that occurs to you, if you choose.

What images, symbols, colors, or sounds come into awareness that might represent your life purpose? Whatever comes to mind or pops into your Love Sphere is perfect.

Consider how continued connection to Field 123 can support you in realigning focus and choices to reflect your divine blueprint. In addition, recognize that Field 123 can also support you in realizing where you may already be living on purpose. This Field is awesome at bringing forth resonant recognition of how we may already have accomplished what we came here to do in many ways, but perhaps we discounted those expressions as seemingly insignificant.

Field 123 activated through the symbol of the pinecone can open us to knowing and living our unique soul-signatures through everyday experiences.

$\mathcal{F}$124

Planetary Balance and Unity.

Field 124 is universal coherence supporting balance on all levels of connection with all of humanity, Earth, galaxies, and interconnected solar systems. Universal Love. Universal Unity.

This Field of universal love and unity supports full recognition of inherent connection to everything and balances the fulcrum of creation back to the harmonic resonance of love: All as One through a field grid template of Sun–Heart–Earth–Galaxies, and Universal Grace as the great equalizer.

This Field supports harmonic resonance and fine-tuning of Schumann's resonance of Earth. Field 124 synchronizes the divine timing of Field 111 with the natural timing of Earth's coherence.

Field 124 supports personal and global coherence by supporting resonance with the knowing-

PICHUGIN DMITRY/SHUTTERSTOCK

ness that all heartbeats can synchronize as One through Love.

Our chosen symbol for this Field is the sun and a palm tree. The sun is a generous, loving, radiating star that eternally shines on us. It represents joy, life, hope, clarity, renewal, vitality, and connection. The sun is pure light.

Similarly, a palm tree has many solar attributes while remaining present and grounded with the planet. The head of the palm with its radiating fronds can be visually compared to the glowing sun-star.

The palm tree is known to have both masculine and feminine qualities and is a beautiful example of unity expressing as duality. Field 124 is a Field of unitary well-being for all life as One, expressing through the many, as distinctions. Nothing is separate, although some things may appear separate. This interconnection and cohesive unity expressing as diversity are supported and restored through resonance with Field 124.

This Field allows for a conscious movement beyond the fear-based notions that the world is on the brink of destruction to a return to loving references supporting unified construction. This Field supports universal coherency, congruency, and integrity in action. Field 124 is a unified breath of life for all living beings of consciousness. Breathe. Just breathe.

Drop down into the field of the heart and center in your Love Sphere. Signal Field 101 for support, if you choose. From the field of the heart, intend to connect to Field 124 and allow for the chosen symbol of the sun to enter your awareness. Connect the sun symbol to your heart field through a beam of coherent white light. Feel the radiance of the sun on your entire being. What sensations or experiences occur for you as you connect to Field 124 through the symbol of the sun and the field of your heart? Write down what occurs to you, if you choose.

While remaining connected to the symbol of the sun and staying centered in your heart, allow for the image of a palm tree to emerge anywhere in your awareness. Notice the connection between the palm tree and the sun and feel the radiance of the sun touching every part of the tree, from the top of its fronds down through its base to the roots that are embedded and united with the soil of the planet. Follow the sun as it radiates beyond the tree roots to the grids and signaling ley-lines that contain the cellular memory of the Earth. See the sun clearing the confusion of fear and desiccation that may be encoded in these planetary information superhighways.

Allow for your awareness and focus to return to the image aboveground of the palm tree. Notice its simple beauty, unified with itself, one with the soil that serves as a foundation and as nourishment for its roots and one with the sun that serves as light for growth. Notice its perfectly imperfect attributes. Perhaps it is tilted to the left or may have more fronds on one side than the other. It doesn't care. It is basking in love's reflection. It is basking in the Joy of Being. May we do the same.

Take a deep breath. Breathe in and let the breath move through you in the same way the sun radiates through every part of the palm tree. On exhale, send love to the sun, the palm tree, and all the interconnected living essences that make up this ever-expanding, ever-evolving universe.

Allow for that limitless love that is within you to project out to all the distant (and not-so-distant) galaxies beyond our solar system. Allow your soul and whole system to connect as love beyond the boundaries of the multiverse and beyond what you may currently be able to sense or imagine.

Breathe in and know . . . All is well. Breathe out and know . . . All is well. Breathe in and circulate love through your interconnected system. Breathe out and radiate love to all interconnected systems. One breath of life, one sun, one heart, and one Tree of Life rooted in the truth of unity.

MASSON/SHUTTERSTOCK

From the field of the heart to the sun, to the grass and trees and all the seas, we are One. WE are One. Just One.

Be One with this notion and open to the ocean of Love that is available, within the field of the heart and everywhere you may choose to go. Wherever you are, these Fields of love support you. Signal the fields freely as you choose, one heartbeat at a time, synchronized to the universal heartbeat of life, in rhythm with all that is love too. Together WE can always choose to PLAY in Fields of Love In-Joy!

Melissa Joy

Melissa Joy Jonsson (M-Joy) is best known for her ability to engage people from all over the world to embrace their True Authentic Power through accessing universal consciousness by playing in the field of the heart. She has a unique perspective on how we are able to experience living joyfully and loving completely from a state of grace.

Melissa has been teaching popular life-transformational seminars around the globe since 2008. She is the founder and instructor of the "M-Joy Of Being" seminar series, a unifying movement in consciousness dedicated to exploring and expanding heart-centered awareness and practical personal empowerment for everyone. Prior to creating a career she loves, she spent almost fifteen years as an executive in the pharmaceutical industry.

Melissa has a bachelor's degree in psychology from the University of California at Santa Barbara. She completed graduate studies at Pepperdine University's Graziado School of Business and Management.

She is sought after as a respected published author and as a frequent guest speaker on global radio broadcasts. Melissa is well known for her eloquent articulation and personal accessibility on both nationally and internationally recognized social media platforms.

Melissa Joy is passionate about inspiring every other person to realize his or her True Authentic Self (TAS) with practical, creative, and powerful wisdom that she embodies every day. She enjoys long runs near the ocean in San Diego, reading, hanging out with friends, and sharing with people the joyful journey of living their infinite potential. To learn more about M-Joy, please visit http://www.mjoyheartfield.com/.

46312145R00081

Made in the USA
San Bernardino, CA
04 March 2017